Fleeing from famine in Connemara

Maynooth Studies in Local History

SERIES EDITOR Raymond Gillespie

This volume is one of six short books published in the Maynooth Studies in Local History series in 2018. Like their predecessors they range widely, both chronologically and geographically, over the local experience in the Irish past. Chronologically they span the worlds of medieval Tristernagh in Westmeath, a study of an early 19th-century land improver, the Famine of the 1840s in Kinsale, politics and emigration in the late 19th century and sectarian rituals in the late 19th and 20th centuries. Geographically they range across the length of the country from Derry to Kinsale and westwards from Westmeath to Galway. Socially they move from those living on the margins of society in Kinsale and Galway in the middle of the 19th century to the politics and economics of the middle class revealed in the world of Thomas Bermingham and the splits in Westmeath in the 1890s. In doing so they reveal diverse and complicated societies that created the local past, and present the range of possibilities open to anyone interested in studying that past. Those possibilities involve the dissection of the local experience in the complex and contested social worlds of which it is part as people strove to preserve and enhance their positions within their local societies. Such studies of local worlds over such long periods are vital for the future since they not only stretch the historical imagination but provide a longer perspective on the shaping of society in Ireland, helping us to understand the complex evolution of the Irish experience. These works do not simply chronicle events relating to an area within administrative or geographically determined boundaries, but open the possibility of understanding how and why particular regions had their own personality in the past. Such an exercise is clearly one of the most exciting challenges for the future and demonstrates the vitality of the study of local history in Ireland.

Like their predecessors, these six short books are reconstructions of the socially diverse worlds of the poor as well as the rich, women as well as men, the geographical marginal as well as those located near the centre of power. They reconstruct the way in which those who inhabited those worlds lived their daily lives, often little affected by the large themes that dominate the writing of national history. They also provide models that others can follow up and adapt in their own studies of the Irish past. In such ways will we understand better the regional diversity of Ireland and the social and cultural basis for that diversity. They, with their predecessors, convey the vibrancy and excitement of the world of Irish local history today.

Maynooth Studies in Local History: Number 135

Fleeing from famine in Connemara
James Hack Tuke and his assisted emigration scheme in the 1880s

Gerard Moran

FOUR COURTS PRESS

Set in 10pt on 12pt Bembo by
Carrigboy Typesetting Services for
FOUR COURTS PRESS LTD
7 Malpas Street, Dublin 8, Ireland
www.fourcourtspress.ie
and in North America for
FOUR COURTS PRESS
c/o IPG, 814 N Franklin St, Chicago, IL 60622

ISBN 978–1–84682–721–1

Printed in Ireland
by SprintPrint, Dublin.

Contents

Acknowledgments

I am indebted for the help and encouragement that I have received from many people and institutions during the study and completion of this work. For many years the work and commitment of James Hack Tuke to the poor of the west of Ireland, and Connemara in particular, had fascinated me, especially as his sympathy and dedication has largely been forgotten and overlooked. Among those who have been an inspiration are those involved in the Tuke Project in Belmullet, Clifden and Oughterard: Rose Marie Geraghty and John Gallagher in Belmullet; Kathleen Villiers-Tuthill and Declan Mannion in Clifden; David Collins and Antoinette Lydon in Oughterard. A special word of thanks to the County Galway Heritage Officer, Marie Mannion, whose support for the project has been unwavering. To all those who have provided me with support and help during my fascination with Tuke I would like to record my appreciation: Prof. Christine Kinealy, Dr Tony Varley, Prof. Gearóid Ó Tuathaigh, Dr Ciarán Ó Murchadha, Dr Caitriona Clear, Prof. Enrico DeLago, Dr Regina Donlon and Dr Raymond Gillespie. A special work of thanks to Prof Catherine Shannon and the late Prof. Lawrence McBride who provided copies of the ship manifests that carried the Tuke emigrants from Clifden and Belmullet, and Dr Ciara Breathnach for providing copies of the Tuke letters, which are located in the University of Limerick Library. I would also like to thank the staff of the Special Collections at NUI Galway, Galway County Library, the National Library of Ireland, the Dublin City Library and the Dublin Diocesan Archive for making their manuscripts available for consultation. I am indebted to the Social Science Research Centre at NUI Galway for the research facilities that have been made available to me. This study is dedicated to the late Betty Ryan, a dear friend and colleague, who had a love of all aspects of Ireland, and in particular of Limerick and Galway. As ever, I am indebted to my wife, Clodagh, and our much loved children, Eoghan, Cian, Cillian and Caoimhe, for giving me stability and a life away from the manuscripts.

Introduction

Throughout the 19th century visitors and tourists to Connemara commented on its beauty and ruggedness, but also highlighted the poverty and wretchedness of its inhabitants. Writers such William Makepeace Thackeray, Mr and Mrs Hall, Harriet Martineau and others wrote of the conditions under which the people lived and their attempts to eke out an existence from a landscape that was harsh and at best marginal.[1] The subsistence existence of the population meant continuously existing on a knife-edge and the slightest change in their circumstances led to food crises and, on occasion, famine. The Great Famine of 1845–52 had devastating consequences for the region and like many parts of the west of Ireland the loss of life when the potato crop failed was immense, but unlike most of the rest of the country population loss was due to high mortality levels rather than emigration.

Throughout the second half of the 19th century, Connemara continued to experience periodic crop failures and famines as the region retained largely pre-Famine structures and the population retained a subsistence existence. While the consolidation of holdings took place in the rest of the country most farms in Connemara continued to be unable to provide the occupants with a living and they had to supplement their incomes through the manufacture of kelp. Emigration was not a feature for the people of Connemara at a time when there was a massive exodus from the rest of the country. This was largely because its inhabitants did not have the resources to fund their emigration.

Push and pull factors determine the level of emigration, but the ability to finance the emigrant's travel, either directly or indirectly, determines when he or she can leave and where they can settle. A noticeable feature of Irish emigration in the 19th century was the pattern of chain migration with family and friends contributing towards the travel of the emigrant, who then settled in locations close to neighbours and relatives from Ireland. As David Fitzpatrick points out, Irish emigration can be seen 'as a complex network of distinct streams flowing from particular regions of origin to particular countries of settlement'.[2] For much of the 19th century migration was not a realistic option for people from Connemara even though many wanted to escape from the perennial poverty and destitution of their area.

While much has been written on the Irish emigrant experience, until recently this has been examined in a national context with little assessment of local contexts and variations. Emigration is an individual experience and each participant has a different story to tell. This is where local history is important as a 'building block' to highlight local features and circumstances that contribute to the overall emigration pattern. What becomes apparent is the sense of place and community that most emigrants brought with them. As they departed one part of Ireland to join up in destinations where friends and relations from home had settled, they developed a community overseas with strong links to the home place in Ireland. The emigrants' 'community of interest' was often centred on the home place in Ireland. As Michael McLoughlin from Achill who settled in Cleveland told his parents, not to worry 'for I feel as if I was at home, for I see more of my friends here than at home'.[3]

Irish emigration in the 19th century was largely associated with those who were young and single. As Fitzpatrick argues, 'emigration became an accepted episode in the life-cycle, akin to marriage or inheritance' and it was as if Irish parents reared their children to leave on the emigrant boat and live the rest of their lives on foreign soil.[4] A pattern within families was established as confirmed by Annie O'Donnell from Spiddal, who at 18 years left for Pittsburgh to join her two sisters, for 'As soon as a boy or girl gets big enough to help the house, he is forced to leave perhaps never again to see those dear ones'.[5] In the post-Famine period few families left although in the 1850s, many were reunited after a separation: fathers emigrated on their own and when they had the resources they sent back the passage fares so their wives and children could join them in North America. The poor law system also permitted payment of passage fares to reunite families.[6] Not until the 1880s did large-scale family emigration take place, facilitated through the assisted emigration scheme of the English Quaker and philanthropist, James Hack Tuke, when 1,500 families from Connemara and Mayo had their passage paid to North America. While sending the young and single held the prospect of remittances being sent back to family and friends in Ireland allowing the possibility of those at home being able to live in relative comfort, the emigration of families would allow the vacated farms to be redistributed among the remaining tenants. It was argued this would create viable farms among the remaining families and provide them with greater prosperity.

Throughout the 19th century, assisted emigration was seen as the panacea for Ireland's problems of poverty, destitution and population congestion, but it was realized that to be successful government involvement was necessary because of the massive numbers that needed to be relocated. It was suggested that sending the Irish poor to the colonies had a number of advantages: there was a demand for labour in places like Canada and Australia, and the Irish could fill this void; at the same time those who left would improve their positions and have a better life.[7] The Peter Robinson scheme from the Blackwater region of north Munster to Peterborough, Ontario, between 1823 and 1825, was the only occasion where there was direct government intervention when it was deeply involved in the whole process.[8] While there were attempts during the Great Famine to persuade the government to fund a major emigration scheme to

Canada as a relief measure, the authorities refused to become involved. The only form of involvement was through the poor law unions.[9] Individuals like Lord Mounteagle in the 1830s and 1840s advocated assisted emigration, and during the Great Famine this was carried out by landlords and their agents, but their motives were mainly economic rather than philanthropic. The experiences of those who left under these schemes was largely negative.[10] Even in the decades after the Famine assisting the poor and the surplus population from congested districts was promoted mainly by individuals who saw emigration as the only pragmatic solution. Among those who advocated assisted emigration were Vere Foster, John Sweetman and James Hack Tuke.

It is surprising that the role of Tuke in Irish history has been largely neglected or confined to his activities in Ireland during the Great Famine given his work and commitment to the poor of the west of Ireland in the 1880s and 1890s. The only major study on Tuke was published in 1896, three years after his death, and compiled by his friend, Sir Edward Fry. This is largely a memoir based on the diary of Tuke's second wife, Georgina, who he married in November 1882, and his letters to his two daughters, Frances and Meta. While Fry's work provides an insight into Tuke's activities in Ireland, it provides little in terms of analysis of his endeavours and placing him in an overall historical context. It is surprising that historians have neglected Tuke's labours in Ireland as he wrote a number of pamphlets and articles on his work in Ireland, and in particular on poverty in the west. His engagement and labours on poverty in the post-1880 period are barely mentioned and his contribution to the Congested Districts Board has not been acknowledged, although Ciara Breathnach in her study of the board does state that the Irish chief secretary, Arthur Balfour, 'has probably been over-credited' with its establishment and the role of Tuke was greater than has been realized.[11] This failure to give Tuke his proper place in Irish history is largely due to the political and agrarian developments that enveloped Ireland during this period, which is unfortunate as his commitment and sympathy to the poor and destitute of Connemara was probably greater than any political and agrarian leader.

1. Connemara and the 'forgotten famine', 1879–81

While the Great Famine was the defining event in 19th-century Ireland, resulting in major economic, social and demographic change, the transformation was not homogenous throughout the country and a two-tier economy came into being. Most parts of the country experienced rapid change and progress, but there were other parts, in particular along the west coast, where this was much slower and pre-Famine structures continued up to the early 1880s. This was especially the case in Connemara. While the population of Connemara was decimated during the Great Famine, unlike in the rest of the country, this was reversed in the following three decades. Between 1851 and 1871 the population of Clifden poor law union increased from 24,349 to 25,231, while in Oughterard it rose from 18,857 to 19,591. The high population density resulted in a major demand for land as there were few economic opportunities available and consequently farm size was small. By 1881, 69 per cent of the holdings in the Clifden union were under 15 acres, with 22 per cent under five acres; while in Oughterard 51 per cent were under 15 acres, with 16 per cent under five acres.[1] Between 1861 and 1881 when farms in the rest of the country were being consolidated, the number of holdings under 15 acres in these unions increased. Some 80 per cent of the farms in Clifden union had a valuation under £4, which meant landlords paid the poor rates, and the average amount of arable land for each family was between 2½ and 3 acres.[2] In his article, 'Emigration from Ireland', published in the *Contemporary Review* in April 1882, the English philanthropist, James Hack Tuke, stated that on one estate in Connemara there were 25 families endeavouring to live on 68 acres of tillage, or 2⅔ acres for each family, while in another case 29 families had 63 acres of tillage, or just over two acres each.[3] The pressure for land in Oughterard union was such that it was exceptional to find a complete holding occupied by a single tenant and many tenants did not hold their farms directly from the landlord.[4] The level of poverty and congestion was also evident in other parts of Connemara: Carna in 1881 had a population of 5,270 comprising 956 families existing on 781 farms, and 175 holdings supported two families on each farm. Only 879 acres of potatoes was grown or just over one acre per family.[5] The electoral division of Lettermore and Garumna in Oughterard union comprised 11,370 acres and had 4,382 inhabitants in 1881; while Crumpaun comprised 8,492 acres with a population of 2,473.[6]

The population survived on a knife-edge by adhering to pre-Famine structures: the subdivision of holdings, a high dependency on the potato as the

main food source, early marriage, and availing of non-agricultural activities
such as manufacture of kelp and returns for seasonal migration. Tenants on the
Law Life Assurance Company estate at Cleggan subdivided their farms, which
resulted in evictions taking place in the 1860s.[7] The uneconomic nature of the
farms meant a heavy reliance on the potato to support the food needs of the
people: in Clifden 4,900 acres of the 10,600 under tillage grew potatoes and root
crops.[8] In the early 1870s kelp production was worth £15,000 in the Kilkerian
region and the tenants on the Blake estate at Bunowen relied on harvesting the
seaweed-based crop to survive as they were unable to make a living from the
land. Agents of companies such as Patterson and Company of Glasgow, Mr
Hazel and Mr Stephens, advanced as much as £100 to each family which was
used to buy provisions and seed potatoes and then repaid when the kelp was
harvested.[9]

Even at the best times the population of Connemara had a precarious
existence. In his report from Camus in early 1880, Tuke stated,

> I wish I could produce that rocky coast and wild miserable village … so
> that English people might realise how in these remote places, so many
> thousands of people are living … I will venture to say no one would think
> it possible that any human being could live or even find [a] foothold on
> this rock-strewn shore … they are a race of wild people, poorly clad, and
> living with the cattle in their houses, often lying on the damp ground on
> hay with them.[10]

In the 1860s and 1870s there were a number of occasions when the crops
failed and the people had to rely on relief for survival. During the crisis of 1862–
3 both Clifden and Oughterard unions were classified as seriously distressed
by the Dublin administration, but the crisis was largely averted through the
intervention of private relief organizations such as the Mansion House Relief
Committee, rather than the state.[11] The level and nature of the distress in
Connemara was highlighted by the Dublin Queen's Council, Caulfield Heron,
who wrote, 'If any traveller wishes to see what conditions the peasantry of the
west are being reduced to, let him visit the village of Lissoughter within a half
mile of Recess. There is a collection of filthy hovels unfit for human habitation.
A few starved creatures creep around them with the wistful look of hunger in
their eyes'.[12] The Mansion House Relief Committee report stated that there
were many parts of the country that regardless of whatever improvements were
made would always be on the edge of want, a clear reference to Connemara.[13]
This was followed in 1866–7 when two-thirds of the potato crop in Clifden
was completely destroyed and the corn was of an inferior quality due to the
continuous rain during the summer; it led to the local guardians stating the
situation was bordering on famine.[14] Crises at a local level continued in the
1870s: Inishboffin and Inishturk were described as congested and the land

just 'barren rocks and little more than a standing place for fishermen and kelp makers'.[15] Inishboffin and Inishturk in the 1870s had a combined population of 1,500 people and had been purchased in the 1850s by Henry Wilberforce from the marquis of Sligo. When Wilberforce got into debt in 1859, J.E. Allies took over ownership. In the ten years to 1880 Allies was owed £935, nearly twice the annual rental, as the tenants were too poor to pay the rent.[16]

While the population of Connemara survived at a subsistence level throughout the 1860s and much of the 1870s, a combination of factors brought about the famine crisis of 1879–81, resurrecting a fear that the calamity of 1845–50 had returned. While the crisis reached its peak in 1879–80 most tenants were struggling over the previous two years because severe weather conditions led to poor harvests. Between 1877 and 1879 £20 million worth of crops had been destroyed and in 1879 the value of the potato harvest was only one-third that of 1876. The spread of blight caused the greatest concern as it rained for two out of every three days during the summer of 1879.[17] Over half the crop was destroyed and the position was worse in Connemara. At the same time the kelp industry was under threat as it faced increasing competition from potash manufactured in Germany. Fifty of the poorest parishes along the west coast lost £50,000 because of the collapse in prices, declining from £7 to £2 a ton. In the Kilkieran area, the sum earned from kelp declined from £15,000 to between £2,000 and £3,000, and in 1880, Captain Digby Morant of the naval service said those people living on the coast of Connemara were the most destitute of all.[18]

While the people had survived the vicissitudes of the previous two years, the combination of events in 1879 meant they could no longer cope. To survive, many were in debt to local shopkeepers and James Berry, a local Fenian and newspaper correspondent, wrote that Connemara was never in a worse state because the people were mired in debt and not in a position to pay it off. One merchant stated, 'At all times most of the people are in debt to the store-keeper, who is the little banker of the district and no doubt charges "full rates" for his small loans'.[19] One merchant in Oughterard was owed £14,000.[20]

The clergy were the first to highlight the approaching crisis in Connemara and warned that unless the government intervened there would be large-scale fatalities. As the leaders of their communities they felt an obligation to write to the newspapers and the authorities in Dublin alerting them to the deteriorating situation.[21] The parish priest of Spiddal, Revd Patrick Lyons, in February 1879 wrote that there was great distress in his parish as a result of the very severe weather.[22] Over the following months priests from other parts of the country indicated that a famine situation was developing and by June 1879 200 priests in the west and south warned that a catastrophe was imminent in the traditional areas of destitution.[23] The same month, 25 priests, led by Revd Peter Dooley, PP of Gort, in the diocese of Galway, which included a number of parishes in south Connemara, adopted a resolution calling on the landed proprietors to make rent reductions 'comparable with the depressed state of the times'.[24] This was followed in November by the clergy in Connemara writing a memorial to the lord lieutenant, the duke of Marlborough, stating there was universal destitution in the region and calling for productive employment to be put in place such as the construction of a railway between Galway and Clifden or the erection of fishing piers along the coast for the protection of fishermen.[25] Others confirmed there was a major crisis in the region. Agnes Eyre of Clifden Castle summed up the situation in north Connemara when she stated, 'Poverty has long since gone beyond measurement by statistics' and indicated the people just accepted their condition as part of everyday life, 'there is no wrath in their eyes; no malice on those lips; no wishes for evil to imaginary evil-doers. The calamity is accepted as beyond human avoidance'.[26] One of the most impartial accounts came from Mitchell Henry, the local MP, who provided much-needed employment for his tenants on his estate at Kylemore and gave a 25 per cent rent abatement. He wrote,

> The people have neither food, nor clothes, nor credit to buy them, nor work to earn them. Black despair is settling down upon the district, and the efforts of the few in this locality who can give employment, are but a drop in the ocean of misery around.[27]

By the autumn of 1879, an agrarian campaign called 'The Low Rent Movement' organized demonstrations throughout the west of Ireland and many speakers highlighted the plight of the people. The meeting in Clifden on 10 September was addressed by Dean McManus, Revd McAndrew, PP, Revd Maloney, PP; Revd Fahy, CC and Mitchell Henry and called on landlords to grant rent abatements. Revd Maloney from Roundstone said that distress was widespread throughout Connemara and told the landlords to come to 'the relief of those tenants who, but, for the mercy of the merchants could not for many years past have remained in their "hovels"'.[28] Among the landlords who provided their tenants with relief during this period were John Kendall of Ardagh Lodge, Clifden; Captain Thomas of Salruck, Killery and Mitchell Henry.[29] However, the majority of landed proprietors failed to provide their tenants with any assistance. Many were absentees and did not witness at first hand the impact of the failure of the potato. Others were reluctant to provide assistance as it would appear they were giving in to the Land League demands. It was left to the clergy to publicize the position of their parishioners and organize practical measures to deal with the crisis. In Oughterard, the clergy, and in particular the parish priest, Revd R. McDonagh, was responsible for establishing a relief committee in the town. At a meeting on 28 December 1879 he requested that shopkeepers and the influential men in the area attend so that they could solicit and receive subscriptions whereby relief could be given to the poor.[30] Only 50 families in the parish were not severely in debt as 80 per cent of the potato crop was completely destroyed.

The role of the clergy in publicizing the near-famine conditions in their parishes had important consequences: it alerted the outside world to an impending disaster. Irish, British and American newspapers sent reporters to Connemara to secure eye-witness accounts of conditions in the region and Clifden became the central location for these operations. The reporters visited the local clergy who outlined the position of their parishioners and directed them to those villages where the people were most in need. The reporters who visited Clifden, Rosmuc, Carna and other parts of Connemara were shocked by what they witnessed, but were even more perturbed when told that these conditions were part of everyday life for the inhabitants. After his visit to Connemara, the American reporter, James Redpath, stated in an article in the *New York Independent* in April 1880, 'There is a famine in Ireland'.[31] William O'Brien of the *Freeman's Journal* was one of the first reporters to visit Connemara in October 1879 and wrote a series of articles outlining the dreadful conditions that he witnessed. From Oughterard he wrote, 'It is time for those who are responsible for the lives of the people to be a-stirring ... Are they going to heed no cry from Connemara until it comes from coffinless graves?'[32]

The government reaction to the reports of famine and destitution was one of prevarication, maintaining there were conflicting signals. While the clergy and newspaper reports highlighted the extent of the distress, Irish landlords and local government officials played down the crisis claiming the Irish exaggerated the levels of distress. Even experienced officials such as Henry Robinson, appointed Local Government Board inspector in 1879 with responsibility for Connemara and Mayo, believed that the situation was not as bad as that portrayed by the clergy.[33] It was argued that the poor law was able to deal with the distress, but the Clifden guardians were not in a position to do so as in December 1879 they had only £12 for the 1,500 people who applied for relief. There were 800 families in Moyrus parish, but they had not enough potatoes to support 100 of them until the following July and few had the resources to buy seed potatoes.[34] At this stage the crisis in Connemara and other parts of the west was overshadowed by the land agitation, which was gaining momentum in the closing months of 1879 and the government was more concerned with the demonstrations and radical rhetoric than the failure of the potato crop. It was only when the Irish Catholic bishops, at a meeting on 24 October, issued a statement about the crisis and called on the government to introduce public works that would benefit the people that the government moved to provide assistance. This was followed by a deputation from the hierarchy consisting of Archbishop Daniel McGettigan of Armagh, Archbishop Edward McCabe of Dublin, Bishop Laurence Gilloly of Elphin and Bishop George Butler of Limerick meeting the lord lieutenant and expressing the fears of the bishops.[35] This paralleled what they had done in 1846–7. At the same time, 70 Irish MPs sent a memorial to Prime Minister Benjamin Disraeli, calling on the government to introduce measures to prevent a calamity in Ireland.[36] The delay by the authorities in Dublin and London meant that valuable time was lost in introducing measures that would have ameliorated the crisis in Connemara and other parts of the west.

While individual clerics such as Dean McManus of Clifden and Revd Patrick Greally of Carna made appeals for help for their parishioners through the newspapers, others, like Revd Newell of Carraroe, made direct pleas in North America. The response did not meet the needs of their communities because requests were being made from all over the country. There was an acknowledgment of an impending crisis from early June 1879, but no attempt was made to establish a central relief committee until the end of that year. In 1880 the Mansion House Relief Committee gave a number of reasons why this happened. First, a perception that the crisis could be overcome if landlords provided rent abatements and merchants did not collect the outstanding debts from the tenants. Second, the private relief committees would be able to attract financial contributions because of their experiences during the Great Famine. Third, improved weather conditions in October appeared to indicate that harvest conditions were improving.[37] Not until December 1879 was there a realization that the situation was rapidly deteriorating and immediate action was required. This prompted the establishment of private relief organizations.

It was not until December 1879 that there was official acknowledgment that there was widespread distress in the country and many areas were on the verge of famine. The duchess of Marlborough's letter to the *Times* (London) on 16 December 1879 outlining the distress in Ireland and the formation of ladies' relief committees played an important role in highlighting the problem and in changing English attitudes. Here was the wife of the Irish lord lieutenant stating in public that a famine situation existed in Ireland, and that private and public intervention was needed. It was the catalyst for the inward flow of donations into Ireland and the Duchess of Marlborough Relief Committee distributed £135,000 for the relief of distress, a large proportion being sent to Connemara.[38] One of the aims of the committee was to provide children at school with a meal of bread and potatoes. It was also decided to devote £30,000 towards the purchase of seed potatoes for distribution among the tenants who had nothing to plant because they had consumed their supply.[39] The crisis would have been greater if the distribution of seed potatoes had not taken place in late spring of 1880.

On 2 January 1880, the Mansion House Relief Committee was established in Dublin by the lord mayor of Dublin, Edward Dwyer Gray, who was proprietor of the *Freeman's Journal*. The committee included Jonathan Pim, John Barrington, eight MPs, members of the landed aristocracy and both archbishops of Dublin. The committee received £181,000 in subscriptions. The impetus for the relief committee came from the mayor of Adelaide who had written to Gray asking, 'Does the present distress in Ireland warrant action being taken here for its relief?' The speed with which money was forwarded to Dublin amazed the Mansion House Relief Committee who said, 'the money collected in remote cities of Australia or New Zealand one week were feeding the famished peasants of Connemara the next'.[40] At its first meeting on 3 January 1880, the Mansion House Relief Committee sent the following telegram to New York, 'Representative committee formed for the relief of distress, solicits aid from American people'.[41]

As the two relief committees were being established the news was that the situation was getting worse. In early December 1879, Dean Patrick McManus of Clifden described the crisis in his parish where the people were without fuel, food and clothing, doomed to the situation of 1847 and 1848 because there was no hope of securing aid from the government.[42] Revd Patrick Greally, the administrator of Carna, wrote a letter on 29 December 1879, providing one of the most graphic accounts of the widespread destitution in his area and which was published in newspapers in Ireland and the United States:

> On Christmas evening several, poor virtuous women – mothers of large, helpless families – came to me in tears asking for God's sake to give them even the price of one meal for the starving children, that they had not even a morsel of the coarsest food for the little ones on the night of universal joy, that they had neither money nor means to procure it; and they would not get a shilling's worth of credit if they travelled all Connemara; and, finally, that their husbands were gone for the last fortnight to England or Scotland to try and earn something to support their families at home.

He added that half of the 800 families in his parish did not have a month's supply of food.[43] One of the first recipients of aid from the Mansion House Relief Committee was Revd James Craddock of Oughterard who was sent £30 because of the level of distress in his parish.[44]

The two main relief organizations adopted different approaches to the distribution of relief. The Duchess of Marlborough's Committee used the poor law union as its main vehicle and its chairman was usually the chairman of the local board of guardians. These committees then distributed money to the local relief committees. The disadvantage of this system was that the size of many unions in places like Connemara made it too bureaucratic for the efficient distribution of relief. The Mansion House Relief Committee took a more direct approach using the Catholic parish structure for distributing its relief. The parish was an easier system to deal with and could avail of the services of local clergymen who were more aware of local conditions. The local relief committee had to include both Catholic and Protestant clergymen, the chairman or vice-chairman of the local board of guardians, the chairman or vice-chairman of the local dispensary committee and the local medical officer.[45] This balance was to ensure the committees represented all sections of the local community and allow an accurate account of the distress to be forwarded. According to J.A. Fox of the Mansion House Relief Committee the accounts 'are virtually under the control, if not always in the custody of the local clergy' and there was no impropriety.[46] In places like Recess and Inverin no local landowners or their representatives sat on the local relief committees as they were absentees and not fully cognizant of poverty levels in their areas.[47] There were also a number of areas in Connemara, such as Clifden, where there was little co-operation between the Catholic and Protestant clergymen, which militated against an efficient relief strategy. James Hack Tuke described the atmosphere as a 'bitter feeling of hostility'. The lack of co-operation between the different religions groups was primarily due to the activities of the proselytizing societies that had taken place over the previous 30 years.[48]

The Mansion House Relief Committee in Dublin forwarded forms to each local committee who applied for funding asking the number of people being relieved, how the relief was to be administered and details of the names of all to be relieved, their occupations and the number in each family. They had done this in previous famines, as in 1821–3 and 1861–3. The main criticism of the relief organizations was that there was little co-ordination between them, although the Mansion House Relief Committee concentrated its efforts on the west and north while the Duchess of Marlborough Committee was more focused on the south. The local committees and individuals tended to look to all groups for assistance: Revd Greally of Carna appealed to both relief organizations as well as the *New York Herald* Relief Fund (which had been established by the proprietor of the *New York Herald*), James Gordon Bennett, the Land League and Archbishop Edward McCabe of Dublin.[49] In many places the relief committees were unable to raise funds locally because of the severity of the distress and were forced to appeal to the wider community and all the relief organizations. One priest told the Mansion House Committee that hundreds of people daily visited him in search of food, but he was powerless to help. Dean McManus of Clifden also appealed to all the relief committees for help for his parishioners: in March 1880 he wrote to the Mansion House Committee for immediate relief because their fate was death by starvation if aid was not provided.[50] Funds were also forwarded to Archbishop John MacHale of Tuam who then distributed them among the poorest parishes in the diocese, many of which were in Connemara.

There were two aspects to the crisis that had to be dealt with: to provide immediate relief to the hungry and to distribute seed potatoes. Tuke estimated that one million people along the western seaboard were in need of relief by the spring 1880 and in Clifden and Oughterard 80 per cent of the population were severely distressed.[51] A longer-term strategy was also required as the tenants had consumed their seed potatoes and now had none to plant. Unless these were provided the crisis would continue into the following year. Thus, the government and the private relief organizations ensured funds were available for the purchase of seed potatoes: one-third of the *New York Herald* Relief Fund and one-fifth of the money from the Duchess of Marlborough expenditure was set aside for this purpose.[52] The government also made £600,000 available under the 1880 Seed Supply Act. However, the sums were not sufficient to meet the demand, highlighting the extent of the problem of many families resorting to consuming their seed potatoes to survive.

With official recognition of the crisis slow in coming, a more objective assessment of conditions in Connemara took place, including by government officials who previously had refused to acknowledge the extent of the problem. These included Henry Robinson, the Local Government Board inspector, who visited the affected areas in Connemara, often accompanied by the local clergy. When he visited the village of Derryvordera, near Recess, with Revd John Connolly, he was shocked by what he saw: the people were living skeletons, scarcely able to crawl and there was not a house with food. He encountered a similar situation near Rosmuc in December 1879 stating, it was 'a lamentable illustration of how people can live with no visible means of subsistence' as the land was so poor they could not grow potatoes and they could not go to England to work as seasonal migrants as the only language they had was Irish.[53] Of the 350 families in the area, only 15 were able to support themselves and the landlord, Richard Berridge, had provided no assistance. At the same time reports were being published by neutral and impartial observers who came to Connemara to report on the distress. These included Revd James Nugent, a Catholic cleric from Liverpool well-known for his philanthropy; James Hack Tuke and the American journalist, James Redpath. When Tuke visited Errismore in April 1880 he reported,

> Some families had a little store of potatoes and others none; in one house … they are just pulling out their hidden store of potatoes. They have not tasted a potato for months, and these the woman have been saving, as she thought, 'the great famine was coming again'. Thanks to the meal given away this has been averted.

At the same time 600 of the 750 families in Kylemore were on the relief lists with Renvyle most affected. On his visit to Camus, Tuke found that no meal had been distributed the previous week 'and several families were sitting round small quantities of the smallest (old) potatoes I ever saw, and with nothing else to eat but them'.[54] He concluded that since subscriptions from the private charities were likely to decline, the relief committees should concentrate their efforts on poor unions such as Clifden and Oughterard rather than continue its operations throughout the west as the people would be in need of aid for several months to come.[55] The records of the Mansion House Relief Committee show the level of contributions declined after June 1880 at a time when requests for assistance increased.[56] In May 1880, the chairman of the Inverin relief committee, Revd P. Mannion, told the Mansion House Committee that the destitution in his parish was so great that 'in a short time several families must inevitably die of starvation unless aided from somewhere or other'.[57]

The relief operations in Connemara were severely hampered by a virtually non-existent transport system, which meant the relief committees and the authorities had great difficulty in evaluating the extent of the distress and this was where the role of the local clergy was so important. The backwardness and remote locations of many communities can be seen in Tuke's comments on one area in Connemara that was so remote that the poor law relieving officer had not even heard of the place and the people did not know that the workhouse or board of guardians existed. When he visited this village he found the people in severe want.[58] The condition of the islanders off the Connemara coast was also perilous. Both Inishboffin and Inisharb were owned by Mr Allies, an English Catholic gentleman, who never raised the rents, never evicted a tenant and never pressed a debtor, although the tenants owed him between two and five years' rent.[59] Even if the land had been given rent free the tenants would have difficulty surviving. As a result of Allies' intercession, Archbishop McCabe sent £100 for the relief of distress on the islands in January 1880 and another £400 was forwarded to Archbishop John MacHale for the islands in his diocese.[60] Additional relief was also provided by the government to the islands. Between February and August 1880 a number of gunboats, including the *Goshawk, Orwell, Valorous* and *Hawk* delivered 856½ tons of Indian meal, 453 tons of seed potatoes, 30 tons of oats and barley and 110 bales of clothing to the islands and coastal communities which included 2,082 families, totalling 13,483 people, in Connemara. In his report, Captain Digby Morant, the senior officer on the *Valorous*, stated, 'I have not the slightest hesitation in stating that had it not been for the exertions of the charitable organizations during the early part of the year, some of the inhabitants of these western districts and outlying islands would have died from starvation' and those living in Connemara were the most destitute.[61]

By June 1880 there was a perception that the crisis had ended and as a result contributions for the relief of distress declined. While there was a general improvement with the 1880 potato crop there were still parts of the country where distress continued because of the poor quality of seed potatoes distributed to the tenants. In some areas it resulted in further relief having to be provided in the spring of 1881. In Clifden union the local guardians had to extend the outdoor relief provisions in February 1881 and in November 1881 they reported the potato crop had almost been completely destroyed with up to half of the families being destitute by the spring of 1882.[62] Similar reports of problems with the potato crop were recorded from Gweedore, Co. Donegal and Loughrea, Co. Galway. While the 1880 harvest was an improvement on that of the previous year, it only supplied enough food to feed the people and did nothing to redress the debts that had been incurred over the previous years. Most farmers wanted to reduce their debts to the shopkeepers as they feared they would require credit from them in the immediate future.[63]

There is little doubt but that the distress of 1879–81 had all the characteristics of a famine, especially in Connemara. There are a number of reasons why it never reached the scale of the late 1840s. First, it was easier to provide relief because alternative foods, in particular Indian meal, were available at moderate prices. Second, the world quickly became aware of the crisis in Connemara from an early stage because of newspaper coverage and the local clergy who publicized the impending calamity. As the American journalist, James Redpath, told an audience in Boston in June 1880, 'Many a lonely village, hidden among the bleak mountains of the west, would have been decimated by famine if the priests had not been there to tell of the distress and to plead for the peasant'.[64] Third, the intervention of the private relief organizations, in particular the Mansion House and Duchess of Marlborough Relief Committees, was imperative in overcoming the crisis. The Mansion House Relief Committee provided relief for 512,625 people during this period.[65] They had a local network to indicate the extent of the problem and at the same time distributed aid in a timely and efficient manner. Without their intervention there would have been many deaths in Connemara.

The famine of 1879–81 indicated only all too clearly the neglected state of Connemara and other parts of the west. The government, the landlords, the poor law and the baronial sessions prevaricated in their responsibilities towards those in need of aid. The government feared that such intervention would create a precedent that would necessitate having to adopt similar procedures during other periods when the potato failed. Over £2 million had been expended on short-term relief measures, but nothing was done to address the fundamental problems that caused the distress in Connemara and elsewhere. The debate now turned to alternative strategies that could be put in place to deal with the perennial issues of destitution and famine in Connemara and elsewhere.

2. James Hack Tuke's tour of the west of Ireland

In February 1880, James Hack Tuke, an English philanthropist and Quaker, arrived in Ireland, sent by the Society of Friends to distribute relief, although Henry Robinson stated that his friend and future Irish chief secretary, W.E. Forster, was instrumental in his visit.[1] The nomination of Tuke was excellent as he had been involved in Quaker relief during 1847 and was familiar with the west and the condition of the poor who lived there. Moreover, his outspoken reports during the Great Famine had criticized the role both of landlords and government and these had brought him into conflict with landowners such as Sir George O'Donel of Newport House.[2] The correspondence and pamphlets of the Society of Friends during this period told more of the conditions in remote areas of the west of Ireland that those from government officials because the Quakers insisted they be published uncensored and unedited. This was to ensure that the opinions of those on the ground, and who witnessed the direct impact of the Famine, were conveyed to the general public and gave an impartial assessment of what was happening in the more remote parts of the country. Thus, Tuke's reports in 1847 were important in giving the opinions of an impartial, though sympathetic outsider: while critical of landlords and how the tenants were treated, at the same time he praised those landed proprietors who helped their tenants such as Lord George Hill in Donegal. This period showed his empathy and sympathy for the suffering poor in Ireland as seen in the following,

> I regret that I feel so incomplete to express or describe the state of total helplessness that those gentle, suffering people are reduced to. Tenants of an absentee landlord are neglected by those who are living in luxury from the rents collected from the wretched people. Their patience is beyond belief.[3]

Following his visit in Ireland in the 1840s, Tuke devoted much of his time to carrying out charitable work for the Society of Friends near his home base at Hitchen, Middlesex, establishing coal clubs, soup kitchens, evening classes and serving as treasurer of the Friends' Foreign Mission Association. In July 1853, he had returned to Ireland with his brother-in-law visiting many of the places he had reported on in 1847, including Letterfrack. While he witnessed improvements in the condition of the people, the main objective of the visit was to report on the education system as he was at this stage advocating greater state involvement in education.⁴ In 1870 he was sent by the Friends to Paris to carry out charitable work during the Franco-Prussian War.⁵ However, from 1880 up to his death in 1896 he devoted much time and energy to the question of poverty and famine in the west of Ireland.

The main objective of Tuke's visit in the Spring of 1880 was to assess the level of distress and deprivation in those areas he had reported on during the Great Famine and to work in conjunction with both the Mansion House and Duchess of Marlborough Relief Committees. He brought £1,200 which had been contributed by friends and asked that it be distributed 'in cases of peculiar suffering or sickness, or for objects outside the scope of the Dublin Funds'.⁶ Prior to leaving for the west of Ireland, accompanied by his nephew, Henry Meynell, Tuke held a meeting in Dublin with the Irish lord lieutenant, Lord Randolph Churchill, and the duchess of Marlborough, in which they outlined the relief works that were taking place and he was told the authorities would afford him whatever assistance he needed during his trip.⁷

During his ten-week tour of Donegal and the west of Ireland Tuke ensured he gathered information from as wide a range of sources as possible in the localities that he visited. These included landlords, clergymen, poor law union officials and representatives from the Mansion House and Duchess of Marlborough Relief Committees. He was not only prepared to secure the information from these groups, but he accompanied them to the villages and townlands to see for himself the extent of the distress. In this way he was able to forward reports that were first-hand accounts, factual, objective and unbiased. He actively engaged with the local clergy and accompanied them to those areas where there was famine. On his visit to Glenties in Co. Donegal, he wrote, 'Though we saw no starvation, so common here in 1847, we could not feel sufficiently thankful that the aid given by the Funds had arrived in time to avert anything like the terrible suffering and death of that year'.⁸ He did see improvements in a number of places, but it was also evident that large parts of Connemara and west Donegal had not improved and retained pre-famine structures such as over population, unviable farms and early marriages. When he visited Falcarragh, Co. Donegal, he was told by the parish priest, 'The land alone will not keep the people. They are too thick on the ground'.⁹ His reports were important as he was able to compare what he saw with what he witnessed in 1847. One feature that he observed was the failure of local landowners to be more proactive in relief operations. In many areas the landlords were absentees and the local clergymen and professional people comprised the local relief committees. They, and not the landed proprietors, were keeping the poor alive.

Tuke's visit occurred when the agrarian and political situation in Ireland was changing as Land League activity in the west of Ireland was at its height. He encountered the radical political landscape as he was in the west when the 1880 general election was called and this was the area where the Parnellite movement was at its strongest. His comments do indicate a rebuke for the protest as it was taking away from the famine crisis, but he also recognized the frustration of the people.[10] As he was about to leave Ireland in April 1880, he concluded there was widespread distress in the areas he had visited, and while the relief committees had averted a major famine, there were many poorer areas where famine condition continued. In July 1882, Tuke confessed that his visit to the west of Ireland in 1880 changed his life and 'began the chapter of my Irish work of which this journey will be a continuation'.[11]

By the end of his visit Tuke realized that radical solutions were needed to overcome the problems of places like Connemara and the provision of relief during periods of distress was not an adequate response to the region's problems. Others, with an intimate knowledge of Connemara, such as Henry Robinson, had the same opinions: the provision of relief and distribution of seed potatoes was not the long-term remedy for the periodic crop failures in the region. The local landlord and MP, Mitchell Henry, felt that giving the people work rather than the provision of food improved their morale.[12] By the early 1880s there was a consensus that alternative employment opportunities were required if the position of the people of Connemara was to be improved. It was agreed that earnings from the manufacture of kelp and remittances from seasonal migration were no longer sufficient for survival. However, the main concern was the unviable nature of the farms in Connemara, which could not support a family. The Bessborough Commission report in 1881 stated that holdings under 15 acres were uneconomical.[13] Tuke supported this view and an article entitled 'Peasant proprietors at home', published in the *Nineteenth Century* in August 1880, indicated his main priority was to help the small holders survive on their farms. Even those who had purchased their holdings under the 1870 Land Act were unable to earn a living from agriculture.[14] Tuke was not convinced that peasant proprietorship was the solution to the problems of places like Connemara and added, 'It must not be forgotten that proprietorship, whether peasant or otherwise, necessarily involves possession of sufficient means to become a proprietor in addition to the requisite capital required for the cultivation of the land'.[15] The farms in Connemara were too small and the quality of land too poor to provide for the people, 'and it is of the utmost importance to recognize the fact that farms under 10, 15, to 20 acres, according to their quality are too small to support a family'.[16]

The agrarian agitation of 1879–82 focused on land reform as a solution to the land problem in Ireland and in the years that followed remained a major objective of Land League and nationalist activists. However, Tuke and others argued that the problems in Connemara and other parts of the west were more fundamental and a more radical approach was required in dealing with issues like poverty, famine and population congestion. Tuke acknowledged that a solution to the land question was needed and in his conclusion in *Irish distress and its remedies*, he called for the '3Fs' and in particular 'Fixity of tenure'. He was advocating the provisions of the land bill that the Gladstone administration was to introduce into parliament in February. Nevertheless, he realized that other approaches were required for Connemara and the poorer areas of the west.

One of the suggestions that Tuke constantly heard during his tour of the west was that emigration should be encouraged so that people could have a better life. The parish priest of Falcarragh told him that 'emigration is absolutely necessary', while another cleric in Connemara said, 'Let the people leave and in every way that may take them out of the slough of poverty and misery in which they are at present sunk'.[17] In his interview with the Bishop Hugh Conway of Killala, he was told, 'Why should we object, if they can obtain one acre of good land in America, which is worth twenty in this country', although Bishop Michael Logue of Raphoe held a different opinion, 'Emigration is the only area English people think of; but it is the short-sighted policy of idleness'.[18] Witnesses at the Bessborough Commission also suggested that assisted emigration be pursued to overcome the perennial problems of poverty and destitution. Emigration was being discussed because of the initiative of Revd James Nugent who in June 1880, at the height of the crisis in Connemara, had arranged for 309 people to be sent to Graceville, Minnesota, where they were provided with farms by the bishop of St Paul, John Ireland. Nugent argued that the removal of a portion of the population of Connemara was the only solution to its problems as its existing agricultural capabilities were unable to sustain the people. Only entire families were to be assisted as this would allow the remaining population have more viable farms. Nugent felt that by helping individuals to leave it would perpetuate the levels of poverty and destitution as the holdings would continue to be small and uneconomic.[19] The Gladstone administration also considered providing funding for emigration. Provisions in the 1881 Land Act allocated £200,000 for families and individuals to leave for the colonies through a loan system. The colonies had to agree to take in the emigrants, but few were prepared to do so and the money went unused. It is significant that Irish nationalists never referred to these provisions, more concerned with the '3Fs' and the impact it would have on agrarian agitation. The migration proposals also had little relevance for the people of Connemara who were so much in debt that leaving for the colonies was not a realistic option. Tuke saw that the proposed land legislation had few benefits for the small farmers,

> To the dwellers of Camus, or Carraroe, with five and twenty miles of alternative huts and boulders, neither peasant proprietorship nor 'fixity of tenure' can be expected to provide remedial measures, and if it be objected that these are exceptional cases, it would not be difficult to bring forward many other locations of which, in varying degrees, the same might be said. For these the only viable means of relief, in the absence of employment, appear to be 'emigration' or 'scattering'.

Tuke was of the opinion that internal migration was too expensive and would leave the tenant in a poorer condition than if he had emigrated.[20] This was reinforced in a letter that Tuke received from an English friend in July 1880 who was visiting Spiddal and Carraroe in which he wrote,

> For poverty and filth this district exceeds anything I had seen or imagined in Ireland; these poor creatures have nothing out of which to make a subsistence but the few acres of land brought into cultivation by themselves from among the stones and rocks which abound everywhere. I only saw one little plot of ground in which it would be possible to work a plough. It is not possible to bring much, if any, more land into cultivation here, the wonder is that any could be found to cultivate that is now cultivated.[21]

Tuke had clearly given deep consideration to using emigration to address the problems of poverty and congestion in Connemara, but realized it needed to be well structured and coordinated. He would have been aware of the problems that the Nugent scheme encountered from the settled population in Graceville and the feeling they were ungrateful for the help provided. By late 1880 the scheme was in turmoil as the emigrants were unsuited to life on the American prairie with little knowledge or experience of the type of agricultural practices needed. Revd John Stephens who had been involved in selecting the emigrants said, in October 1880, that he had received letters from some of the Connemara emigrants who would gladly come home to Connemara and reclaim bog if they could.[22] Tuke was advocating that families should be assisted as this would free up land and lead to the consolidation of farms into economic holdings for those who remained. There should be a careful and systematic supervision of those who left, not only in Ireland, but continued by properly qualified agents in the destinations they were sent to.

In September 1880, Tuke had meetings with the Irish chief secretary, W.E. Forster, and the resident minister in Ireland for the Dominion of Canada, Sir Alexander Galt, at which emigration to Canada was discussed. Shortly afterwards he set out for North America with two of his daughters on a fact-finding mission and among the places he visited were Baltimore, Philadelphia, Ottawa, Toronto, Washington, Iowa, Minnesota and Manitoba. Among those he consulted with in relation to assisted emigration were the Canadian prime minister, J.A. McDonald; President Hayes of the United States; the governor general of Canada, Lord Lorne; Archbishop Tache of Boniface, Manitoba; and Bishop John Ireland of St Paul.[23]

During the crisis of 1879–81 the Canadian government issued a memorandum in 1880 proposing that it would engage in 'a systematic immigration from Ireland' as a way of relieving distress in the country, but insisted that those who came should not become a burden on the state. Family emigration was to be the solution to the problem of distress and over-population. It was suggested the families be sent to Manitoba and the North West Territories where land was available and the Canadian authorities would look after the emigrants until they harvested their first crop. Emigrants were to receive 160 acres and contribute £2 towards this.[24] To ascertain the potential for emigration to Canada and the mid-west Tuke spent three months in the area and became convinced emigration was a practical solution to the problems of Connemara and the west coast; emigrants should be directed to Manitoba because of its vast potential and the demand for labour.

In an article 'Irish emigration', published in the *Nineteenth Century* in April 1882, Tuke argued that the state should assist people to emigrate from the poorest parts of Ireland, as this would improve the position of those who left and those who remained. There were provisions under the poor law legislation which empowered the guardians to provide the poor with assistance to emigrate. While up to 25,000 people were helped to leave in the 1850s, in particular to Canada and Australia, by the early 1880s this was down to a trickle; in the 1870s only 460 left annually.[25] In the early 1880s it was again argued that it was cheaper to pay the passage fares of families to North America than for them to remain in the workhouses. Tuke claimed that the cost of keeping a family in the workhouse for a year was £50 and this would pay for them to be settled in North America and it would not be a recurring financial burden on the poor law system.[26] This argument had merits during periods when the potato failed and numbers entering the workhouses increased. Tuke suggested for an outlay of £100,000 annually 180 families could leave. He felt that all avenues were closed to the poorer classes in places like Connemara and this only exacerbated the problems of poverty, destitution and population congestion. The people did not have the resources to leave and were forced to continue their subsistence existence. Even if they sold everything they possessed they were unable to raise the necessary funding towards their emigration costs.[27]

Compared to the other assisted emigration schemes then in operation, Tuke's approach was more radical. The Nugent scheme was a knee jerk reaction to the famine crisis in 1880 and the emigrants were ill suited to a life on the prairie. While Nugent was well intentioned and hoped to provide a better future for the people from Connemara, the scheme was poorly planned and executed.[28] John Sweetman's project to Curry, Minnesota, targeted tenant farmers with capital, but was also a failure.[29] The Vere Foster scheme targeted single young females, many of whom came from Connemara, and who were given a £2 voucher, but this did not address the issue of families with uneconomic holdings.[30] While Tuke's proposals concentrated on family emigration, he was more aware of what poor emigrants could expect in North America after his travels to the mid-west and Canada in 1880. The families would not be concentrated in one area and would be spread over a large number of destinations. Sending out whole families was essential for the scheme to be successful, but it created certain difficulties. It was important that the families did not have too many dependent children, otherwise it would mean transferring them from poverty in Ireland to a similar state in North America. It meant the selection process for those who wanted to leave favoured those with sufficient breadwinners to support the family. Those with four to five children under eight years old would not be accepted.

Tuke's proposal of emigration as a solution to poverty and famine was important as he was highly regarded in both Britain and Ireland, and had the political connections and contacts with the establishment to ensure his suggestions were given a fair hearing. There were those who had previously advocated such schemes, but they were largely ignored by government officials. However, Tuke had more influence and this became evident after the publication of his article 'Irish emigration' in February 1881. This was when Gladstone's land bill was being formulated and clause 32 set aside the funds that would allow for emigration to the colonies 'especially of families from the poorer and more thickly populated districts of Ireland'.[31] However, this clause was never invoked because of opposition from the Irish Parliamentary Party.

Throughout 1881 and early 1882 Tuke held discussions with a group of friends, including W.E. Forster, William Rathbone and Samuel Whitbread, about the possibility of initiating a family emigration scheme using voluntary funding.[32] Rathbone and Whitbread were responsible for organizing the meeting that took place at the home of the duke of Bedford at 81 Eaton Sq., London, on 31 March 1881. Over 100 politicians and other figures were invited to attend the meeting.[33] The attendance included eight MPs including H.S. Northcote, Henry Cowper and W.H. Smith who became chair of the committee. Its main objective – to facilitate family emigration – had the support of the Irish chief secretary, W.E. Forster, who in a letter to the duke of Bedford on the day of the meeting stated the committee had his full support and agreed to provide £250 towards its operations and if required this would increase to £500. Forster outlined a number of issues that were incorporated into the committee's programme and suggested it concentrate its efforts on specific areas of the west of Ireland rather than deal with the whole region. He also said the government could not finance the scheme since 'To give the money of the general taxpayer for even so good a purpose as this could be a dangerous precedent' and suggested that the emigrant should contribute part of the passage fare.[34] Tuke in his address to the meeting outlined the advantages of assisted emigration and insisted that families should be sent. His passion for the project can be seen in that the fund became known as 'Mr Tuke's Fund', and resulted in £8,000 being subscribed on that night. By June 1882, over £9,600 had been collected with the largest contributions coming from the duke of Bedford and duke of Devonshire (£1,000 each); W.E. Forster, William Rathbone and Gurney Barclay (£500 each). The committee instructed Tuke to leave for the west of Ireland and implement the emigration proposals and he left on 4 April.[35] He was aware of the enormous responsibility he was being asked to undertake and wrote that it is 'A feeling akin to dread, a feeling endangered by the magnitude of the task naturally sobers my rejoicing'.[36]

3. Tuke and the emigration schemes from Connemara

After arriving in Dublin on 4 April 1882, Tuke immediately went to work holding meetings with John Sweetman, Henry Robinson, Vere Foster, Archbishop John Lynch of Toronto, Edward Dease (the former MP for Queen's Co. who had been a member of the Bessborough Committee), and others. He discussed the advantages and disadvantages of assisted emigration and was worried whether the poor law unions would take out loans for emigration purposes which would have to be repaid over a seven-year period. Tuke also discussed with Archbishop Lynch the proposal to bring Irish families to Manitoba and provide them with farms.[1] He then proceeded to Clifden where the Tuke Committee had decided to initiate the emigration scheme because the local board of guardians on 22 February 1882 had passed a unanimous resolution in support of emigration, agreeing to apply for a £2,000 loan from the Board of Works. The resolution stated,

> That taking into consideration the poverty and destitute condition of the poorer classes of tenantry of this union, particularly those evicted for non-payment of rent, and also those along the sea-shore holding miserable patches of land caused by the subdivision of holdings, and who for three-fourths of the year are in a state of semi-starvation, we respectfully request the interference of the Government to assist in the way of emigration.[2]

Tuke realized that for the emigration to be successful local support and involvement was necessary. In 1847, he had visited local clergy in parishes where starvation was greatest and again in 1880 the priests had brought him to those areas with the greatest distress. As Major D'Arcy, a poor law guardian in the Clifden union, told the Poor Relief Inquiry in December 1886, 'The clergy were the best persons who knew the state of the country best'.[3] When he arrived in Clifden he made personal contact with all of the local Catholic clergy and also attempted to have a meeting with Archbishop John McEvilly of Tuam. The archbishop's support was vital as it would lead to greater clerical involvement. However, it is unclear if this meeting took place.[4] While many clerics supported the emigration proposals and gave Tuke their full co-operation, such as Revd Greally in Carna, Revd McAndrew of Letterfrack, Revd Kane of Rosmuc and Revd Stephens, others opposed any exodus from their districts as a loss of parishioners would lead to a loss of parochial contributions and they feared for the religious well-being of their flocks when they settled in North America.[5] To counteract these objections, Tuke proposed that Catholic priests would accompany the emigrants on their journey and ensure they went to the correct destination after they disembarked in North America. In some cases Catholic priests did travel with the emigrants including Revd Michael Mahony from Preston who left on the *Nepigan* on 31 March 1883 from Galway to Boston and subsequently was assigned to a parish outside St Paul and monitored how the emigrants in Minnesota fared. The 430 emigrants who left Galway on the *Winnipeg* on 19 May 1882 were accompanied by Revd J. O'Donnell, the Catholic chaplain of the Liverpool workhouse.[6]

Tuke was not overawed by the opposition from some of the local clergy who in the initial stages were not overly vocal. He had one encounter with a priest who was opposed 'to the departure of his miserable people – fully admitting the impossibility of the people to live on their holdings at the same time'.[7] While clerical support was important, Tuke realized the majority of the people wanted to leave and a week after arriving in Clifden he stated that despite the opposition of some priests, 'it cannot prevent hundreds asking for assistance to emigrate'.[8] In his report in June 1882, Tuke said of the local clergy, 'Some priests have openly encouraged the work, some have privately sympathized with it, while others have been hostile to it, their opposition has had no apparent effect'.[9] A small group of priests publicly opposed the emigration, but privately corresponded with the Tuke Committee asking for support for individuals to leave. Nevertheless, the success of the scheme in 1882 was primarily due to the engagement of the local clergy who co-operated fully with the committee and persuaded many of their parishioners to apply to be sent to North America.[10]

In the days after his arrival, Tuke encountered a deluge of petitions and letters, from priests, landlords, agents and others, for people wanting to leave. It replicated the experience of Vere Foster who reported the demand to leave was great among the local population,

> There is at present a desire, amounting almost to a mania to emigrate to America, but they are without the means of gratifying their desires, while the demand for female domestic servants and for labourers and mechanics in America is practically illimitable.[11]

Within an hour of Tuke arriving in Clifden he had been approached by a priest stating he knew of 15 families who wanted to leave and by mid-April over 300 people, one-fifth of the population of the town, had applied. The relieving officers who had visited the Berridge estate in Roundstone and Mrs Blake's tenants in Renvyle brought lists totalling nearly 1,000 people wishing to be assisted and said there were as many more who would leave.[12] Tuke related one encounter with a woman who burst into tears when he told her he did not have the time to interview her and she told him, 'we are starving, sir, have pity on the baby, will you not put us on?' It led Tuke to tell his daughters, 'The poverty of these people is really terrible'.[13] The majority of the people saw emigration as their only salvation as they were disheartened with the failure of the potato crop over the previous five years. Most were in arrears with their rent and saw little prospect of this being paid.

While the principal aim behind the Tuke scheme was the removal of the surplus destitute population, he now had to contend with another group who needed to be dealt with immediately for the emigration to attain its goal. Throughout 1881 and 1882 the number of families being evicted increased as landowners cleared their estates of insolvent tenants unable to pay their rent arrears. Prior to Christmas 1881 up to 80 families had been evicted from the Berridge estate and they had no future prospects. They were surviving on the little relief supplied under the poor law and while they offered the landlord one year's rent he had refused because they owed three years.[14] Large-scale clearances also took place on Charles Blake's estate at Bunowen at the very time that Tuke was in Clifden. Among those turned out were Mary McDonagh, Mary Sweeney, Peter Burke, Val Cloherty, John Coyne, Pat Duane, Mary McNamara and Monica King. By this time a total of 150 families were evicted in the Clifden area.[15] A correspondent to *The Nation* wrote in June 1882 after evictions had been carried out in the Oughterard and Carraroe areas, 'The whole country around here appears as though a conquering army had passed over the land, leaving ruined desolation behind'.[16] For the evicted, the poor law was their only support, but this only increased the financial burden on a system in crisis after the famine conditions of 1879–81. This was the reason why the Clifden Board of Guardians had passed a resolution in favour of emigration on 22 February.

Tuke was made aware of the problem of the evicted families during his first week in Clifden, being brought to the hovels that the dispossessed had carved out wherever they could. They had either drifted into Clifden or were squatters on the surrounding bogs and mountains. It was quickly realized that they were most in need of help, but the least promising subjects for emigration. Working closely with officials of the Clifden union he visited Roundstone, Carna, Cashel, Letterfrack and Renvyle encountering evicted families who wanted to emigrate as they felt they had no future in Connemara. Tuke showed a sympathy for these poor people who waited in the pouring rain for his arrival when he visited evicted families in Letterfrack. One man who had six children, one of whom had recently been born, 'ran into his bog hole for an old coat to put on my shoulders'.[17] He came across one family who had sold the timber that formed the back of the house in order to buy meal and replaced it with sods of turf. They had nothing else to sell and 'starvation stared them in the face'. Eight people were living in this hovel and the wife was expecting a baby. The only furniture was a small wooden box and the roof was very low. In another cabin Tuke came across a family who lived in a filthy and dark hovel except for a slight opening in the roof which served as a chimney and gave some light.[18]

It did not take him long to realize that these families needed to be assisted as otherwise the success of the whole project would be undermined. All of those who were evicted informed Tuke that they wanted to emigrate, but did not have the resources to do so.

It was decided that the emigration scheme should be put in place as quickly as possible in order that the emigrants could arrive in North America in late spring and be able to settle and secure employment. However, within days of his arrival Tuke had to contend with another crisis that threatened to derail the project. The Clifden guardians decided to rescind the loan application for emigration so that the Tuke Committee now had to bear the full cost of the operation, well above the financial outlay it had envisaged.[19] The guardians' decision to withdraw their involvement indicates how emotive the issue of emigration was. While their resolution on 22 February in favour of emigration and to apply for the loan indicates the importance they placed on emigration as a remedy to the region's problems, their withdrawal from the project suggests economic arguments took precedence. Many who were applying to leave had received loans under the 1880 Seed Supply Act and there were fears these would not be repaid if they emigrated as they were unable even to contribute towards their passage fares. The union was under severe financial pressure in 1882 because many ratepayers were unable to pay their rates resulting in cheques not being honoured by the banks. By early 1883 it had debts of over £2,000.[20] There is also the possibility that the guardians wanted to let the Tuke Committee finance the scheme as it appeared to have sufficient resources. One group in particular were very much opposed to the people leaving for North America. These were the shopkeepers, some of whom were poor law guardians, who felt the scheme would have a negative impact on their businesses and many of the applicants owed them money. A deputation met Tuke in Clifden within two weeks of his arrival and while happy to see the evicted assisted, they wanted others struck off the lists. Shopkeepers undoubtedly played a role in the guardians' decision to rescind the loan application.

The guardians' decision resulted in Tuke having to devote all of the committee's resources and energy to the Clifden area to the exclusion of other parts of the west where he had hoped to provide assistance. In April, Tuke had visited Mulranny, Co. Mayo, where he was approached by 300 people from the area and from Achill who wanted to be assisted, but he was unable to include them in the scheme. There were other areas of conflict between Tuke and the guardians. While the guardians had agreed to apply for the loan they were not prepared to spend the money in a way which the Tuke Committee deemed to be satisfactory. For an outlay of £4,000 they wanted to assist 1,000 people, which the committee regarded as inadequate. No provision was made to send the emigrants to their destinations after they disembarked at the American ports and they would not be provided with suitable clothing for the journey. Tuke at this point was 'waiting on tenter-hooks to know what decision the Board has come to' which meant a delay in sending out the emigrants.[21] In many ways the guardians wanted to replicate the assisted emigration schemes which many landlords had put in place during the Great Famine and which had created much adverse publicity and criticism.[22]

In addition to the challenges that Tuke had to deal with in selecting and interviewing the applicants and putting structures in place for families to leave, he was also compelled to keep the committee in London informed as to what was taking place and secure their approval for any changes that had to be put in place.[23] This was especially the case after the guardians had withdrawn their loan application. The committee decided to continue the project, but scaled it back compared to the original aims, largely due to Tuke's urgings.

The pressure on Tuke was immense: besides making the travel arrangements both in Connemara and North America, he had to select those who were to be sent, provide adequate clothing for the journey, and arrange departure times for the ships. The scheme could not have been conducted without the assistance and co-operation of those at a local level, such as clergymen and relieving officers, as well as friends who came to assist Tuke. These included Major W.P. Gaskell, who had experience of relief work in Connemara with the Duchess of Marlborough Relief Committee, and Captain Robert Ruttledge-Fair, a Local Government Board inspector and a native of Co. Mayo. At a local level he was assisted by John Burke, the clerk of the Clifden union; the relieving officers, Pater King, Stephen Joyce and Mr Berry; and medical officials such as Dr Gorham of Roundstone and Dr Kearney of Carna.

Guidelines were provided to the relieving officers in relation to the selection of the emigrants. Each family should have a certain number over 12 years of age who were counted as workers to ensure the family would not become a burden on charities in North America. At least one family member had to be able to speak English. While the initial aim of the Tuke Committee was that emigrants would provide half of the travel cost, it was soon apparent that the vast majority of applicants could contribute nothing as they came from the poorest electoral divisions: Bunowen, Cleggan, Errislanan, Inishboffin and Selerna.[24] At an early stage Tuke investigated the possibility of using local ships to transport the emigrants to North America, travelling to Westport to discuss fares and ships with the shipping agent, Mr Malley, but settled with the Allen Line who were prepared to divert their ship from Glasgow to Galway to pick up the emigrants.[25]

Over a three-week period, from 28 April to the 19 May, the Tuke Committee succeeded in sending 1,267 people to Boston and Quebec on three ships, the *Austrian*, the *Nepigan*, and the *Winnipeg*. Three hundred came from the town of Clifden and district, 433 from Errismore, 350 from Roundstone and 183 from Letterfrack and Renvyle. While the arrangements were well organized and executed, inevitably there was confusion and mayhem on the days the emigrants were to travel, mainly caused by the people themselves. Arrangements were made to bring the emigrants by coach from Clifden to Galway. When the *Nepigan* left Galway on 4 May there were those who did not want to leave, while people appeared who had not been selected, but wanted to travel. Others arrived in rags although the committee had provided £5 per family to purchase new clothes. Those travelling on the *Austrian*, which left Galway on 28 April, were given packets of tea and sugar by Tuke which he had received from a friend. Blankets had to be secured in Galway just before the group departed. Again, the committee had to provide between £3 and £6 to each family for clothing.[26] All assisted in 1882 had been evicted from their farms. An examination of those who left on the *Nepigan* provides an indication of those sent to North America. It comprised 350 people. Six of the heads of family were over 50 years with two, Matt Mullen and Patrick Murray, over 60. The largest family was that of P. Connolly, who left with his wife and eight children who ranged in age from 20 to one. In some cases the criteria of the number of working children was not applied as with John Keane who was accompanied by his wife and three children, aged six, four and one.

The sheer scale of the undertaking was massive, but how it was expedited was impressive. Within six weeks of its formation, the Tuke Committee had succeeded in organizing and sending nearly 1,300 people to North America. No structures were in place when he arrived in Clifden, yet within three weeks the first group had been sent to Boston on the *Austrian*. The pressure on Tuke can be seen after the second group left Galway for Quebec when he told his daughters, 'In a fortnight another counterpart must be ready and the amount of labour ... in selecting and arranging and the details connected therewith are really tremendous'. Certain misgivings are evident in his correspondence as the third and final group were about to leave on the *Winnipeg*.

While Tuke endeavoured to encourage the emigrants to settle in Canada where the authorities were prepared to look after them, the preference of most was to be sent to the United States where they had friends and relations. He was pragmatic enough to realize there was no point in forcing them to a country they were reluctant to go to. Tuke was also aware that while they could be sent to Canada they would probably cross the border into the United States at the first opportunity. Most who left for the United States in 1882 settled in Pittsburgh with a few going to Minnesota and Wisconsin.[27] Only one family went to Canada of the first group that left on the *Austrian*. But this increased to ten families, or 56 people, with the *Nepigan*. When the *Winnipeg* departed on 19 May, this had increased to 170 persons, reflecting the desire of the poor of Connemara to be sent anywhere rather than remain in Ireland.[28] However, Tuke was exasperated and disappointed that he had not been able to help more to leave and wrote to his daughter, Frances, 'it is very hard to refuse thousands of people who are begging to go, when one knows that the money is there for a certain number at any rate'. He was also unhappy that the committee proposed to ask each emigrant to contribute £3 towards their passage when they had nothing,

'Think of asking a beggar who asks for a penny to show that he deserves it by giving you a half crown!'[29]

Tuke's work in Connemara in 1882 went largely unnoticed nationally. This was mainly because the country was engrossed in political and agrarian agitation as Parnell and the other Land League leaders were imprisoned in Kilmainham jail. While he was conducting his interviews in Clifden the 'No Rent Manifesto' was issued by the incarcerated leaders urging the tenants not to pay their rents and the Phoenix Park murders occurred two days before the second group of emigrants sailed on the *Nepigan*, when the new Irish chief secretary, Lord Frederick Cavendish, and the under-secretary, Thomas Burke, were assassinated by the Invincibles. A political crisis ensued so the events in Clifden were largely ignored. It was not until the Arrears of Rent Act was debated in the House of Commons in June 1882 that the Irish Parliamentary Party MPs asked who was this 'Mr Tuke' to which W.H. Smith and Samuel Whitbread said, he 'had been distinguished for philanthropy in all parts of the world'. Tuke himself was not happy with this fame and told his daughters, 'I think a great deal too much has been said about my little bit of work and I hope it is all over now'.[30]

The Clifden project in 1882 was in many ways an experiment to determine the logistics and procedures in how an emigration scheme would work. When it ended in May 1882 a number of issues were evident. First, the demand for emigration in Connemara was greater than the resources available to a private organization. When the 201 people left on the *Austrian* it had cost the committee £1,315 or £6 11s. 8d. per person. £885 was spent on ocean passages, £125 for American railway fares, £125 for clothing, £75 for conveyance to Galway and £125 for other incidentals.[31] To continue with assisted emigration and deliver on its objectives, government funding was necessary as it was beyond the capabilities of a private organization like the Tuke Committee. Second, the participation of the North American authorities was essential for the successful integration of the emigrants when they arrived at Boston or Quebec. Those who arrived in Quebec in 1882 on the *Nepigan* and the *Winnipeg* were looked after by Canadian government agents, while those who disembarked at Boston were taken care of by Tuke's friends and forwarded to the various destinations for settlement. In his letter to the committee on 12 June 1882, Tuke's assistant, Major W.P. Gaskell, said of the emigrants,

> [They seem] delighted to go; and their bright countenance, fine physique, and respectable appearance convey the impression that their transfer ... cannot fail to assure to them a life materially better than they have been accustomed to lead at home.[32]

Tuke also received correspondence stating that the families sent to Toronto had settled in well, but the situation was 'not quite so satisfactory' with some of those who settled in Wisconsin.[33]

The Clifden scheme showed that a solid foundation had been established for future emigration and the structures could be extended to other parts of the west of Ireland. As the Tuke Committee stated in its June 1882 report, 'the Committee are convinced that a vast amount of work in the way of emigration still needs to be done'.[34] Systematic emigration was seen as the only hope for the excessive population of places like Connemara and Tuke added 'I am ... more than ever assured that it is the immediate and imperative duty of the government to take up and investigate the condition of the western unions, and adequately and promptly to deal with their special circumstances'.[35] Some adjustments needed to be put in place with procedures. Lists sent to Tuke from some areas to be adjudicated on provided full information regarding the applicants, but others were poor, which held up the proceedings. The list from Scannive gave no real information on individuals or families, or the proportion of those of working age in each group.[36]

The Tuke Committee was prepared to use its political connections in order to advance the emigration agenda. Just after it published its report in July 1882 a deputation met the new Irish chief secretary, Sir George Trevelyan, and impressed upon him the need for government involvement, in particular that public funding be made available for emigration.[37] Throughout the period that the Tuke emigration schemes were in operation, Tuke was prepared to use his political and business connections to promote and advance the project. He was constantly meeting with people like W.E. Forster, W.H. Smith, William Rathbone and other MPs, members of the Athenaeum Club, where he was a member, and business people. No opportunity was lost to promote and secure support for the venture illustrating his dedication and commitment to the scheme. The petition that was sent to the government included the signatures of fifteen members of British society including the duke of Bedford, Samuel Whitbread and W.E. Forster.[38] During the summer of 1882 Tuke played a prominent role in the drafting of the emigration clauses that were to be included in the Arrears of Rent Act. It was decided that all emigration under the new legislation should be 'nearly free'.[39] In July the Tuke Committee was asked to administer the scheme in those unions 'which are too poor to borrow or raise any money. This is very much what we asked'.[40] The government's decision to provide funding was regarded by Tuke as a major achievement as Gladstone had initially indicated that it would not contribute towards emigration and the Irish Parliamentary Party was totally opposed. The victory led Tuke to state, '[It] is a great one for the committee to have induced the government to change its point so suddenly. Let us hope amidst it all that some good will be done – some suffering alleviated ... and discontent allayed'.[41]

An intense debate within government took place in relation to the emigration scheme. It was argued that the money used for the relief of distress during 1879–81 was wasted as it made no fundamental difference in improving the position of the people in the poorest parts of the country. Unlimited funding for relief, seed potato supply schemes or the issuing of grants to distressed poor law unions was no longer regarded as prudent by the authorities and a more radical approach was required. In 1886, Henry Robinson stated, 'Never was money more easily obtained, and never I fancy, did it fail more lamentably in its objective'.[42] Tuke's assisted emigration scheme appeared to be the solution as it removed a large section of the most destitute population. When the emigration clauses of the Arrears of Rent Act were debated in July 1882 most English MPs supported the sending of the poor to North America as the panacea to the perennial problems of poverty, distress and population congestion in the west of Ireland. Consequently, the government allocated £100,000 for state-aided emigration under the Arrears of Rent Act. Forty-two unions along the west coast were provided with funding, with the government contributing £5 towards each emigrant and the poor law unions gave the rest[43] though a number of unions were regarded as being too poor to provide the additional funding. The Tuke Committee was asked to administer the scheme in Clifden and extend its operations to Oughterard, Belmullet and Newport unions. The committee had already shown its expertise and capabilities in administering large-scale emigration in one of the poorest unions. The committee now covered a region with a combined population of 46,000. The government was to provide £26,445 to the Tuke Committee, but it had to come up with an additional £12,049: £8,443 came from private donations and it also received the remaining money from the Duchess of Marlborough Relief Committee Fund, which came to £3,600.[44]

After the emigration clauses in the 1882 Arrears of Rent Act were confirmed Tuke returned to Connemara in July 1882 and was convinced 'that emigration is the absolute necessity of this impoverished district' after visiting a number of villages. He interviewed families in Carna in their 'houseens' and described what he witnessed,

> These 'houseens' are little spaces of 2 to 3 feet deep and 10 to 12 long by 6 to 8 wide dug out of the bog against some large stones which serve as a wall on one side and the sods cut out for the other walls and rood, and in these literally big holes in which a tall man cannot stand upright are scores of families, men, women and children. One woman expecting to be confined very shortly – she had fallen down and hurt her back badly against a rock and was in much pain. She had a 'wake' husband and 5 or 6 children. In another a sick child lay on some straw on bare-earth – in another two little misshapen half starved orphans were living. But worse than all it is I think to see fine strong men asking for work or help to emigrate, sitting crouching in their hunches over a bit of peat fire which fills the air with blinding smoke who have no hope, nothing left but to brood over their misery. How I long for a few thousand pounds to help them to emigrate and place them beyond the reach of want or wretchedness.[45]

Under the Arrears of Rent Act people had to apply before 31 January 1883 and 6,420 looked for assistance from those unions administered by the Tuke Committee. The successful applicants were to be informed ten days before they were due to leave. This was to ensure that the tenants would sow a crop and have something to fall back on if their application was unsuccessful. A fear existed that tenants would not cultivate their holdings and thus force the Tuke Committee to send them to North America. Some tenants did sell all their possessions and vacated their farms although they were not officially informed they had been selected to leave. The alternative that the Tuke Committee faced was to leave them in Connemara where they would inevitably become a financial burden on the poor law and thus defeat the fundamental concept behind the emigration scheme. It was thus imperative that the selections were carried out at a time that would allow the people return to their holdings and plant a crop which would feed their families. The emigration would commence before the end of March and continue until the end of June.[46] The committee was reluctant to send emigrants to the eastern cities of the United States unless encouraging letters, including stamped envelopes, were provided from friends and relations who were already settled there and who promised to provide for the emigrants when they arrived. In February 1883 Tuke commenced the selection process in Connemara.

Those centrally involved in the emigration programme met at the Shelbourne Hotel, Dublin on 12 February. They included Tuke and his wife, Georgina, whom he had married the previous November; Howard Hodgkins, Mr and Mrs Sydney Buxton, and John Sweetman and his wife. They also had consultations with Henry Robinson of the Local Government Board; Earl Spencer, the lord lieutenant; Mr Hamilton, the under-secretary and Mr Jenkinson of the Criminal Investigation Department.[47] At this stage it was decided to separate the administration of the unions under the Tuke Committee's control and while Tuke continued in charge of Clifden, Major Gaskell was in control in Oughterard, and Sydney Buxton was appointed to Belmullet and Newport. This was to expedite matters as the selection, interviewing and transport of the emigrants was time consuming and the geographical extent of the four unions vast. Among those who came to assist Tuke in Clifden were Henry Hodgkins and Mr Higgins.

The Tukes arrived in Clifden on 20 February and immediately set to work through lists of applications from Bunowen, Selerna and Errislannan with the relieving officers John Burke and Peter King. The interviewing process took place in centres such as the dispensary at Letterfrack, the hotel in Carna and the guardians' boardroom in Clifden. Three people were usually involved in the interviews: Tuke, a relieving officer or medical officer and the local priest if he was available. When the list for the Carna area was examined on 22 February Tuke worked with Dr Kearney, the local medical officer and Mr Berry, the relieving officer; in Letterfrack in March among those who examined the applications were Revd McAndrew, PP; Stephen Joyce and Peter King, both relieving officers. It led Tuke's wife, Georgina, to state, 'Hard, anxious work this selecting is, and we had so many applications that could be granted for the steamer of the 23 [March]'.[48] The work was onerous and time-consuming. When the interviews started at the Letterfrack dispensary on 19 February in the presence of Henry Burke, he found that many of the applicants were former kelp workers who had fallen on hard times. The building was full and many could not speak English so the relieving officers had to be used as translators. The interview process took over four hours.[49] Similar scenes occurred at Clifden, Carna, Renvyle, Leenaun, Ashleigh and other centres. When Tuke arrived in Carna on 27 February the hotel was crowded with up to 400 people wanting to emigrate. Georgina Tuke recorded as the families were being interviewed, 'They were simply wild to go, "to be out of this miserable country", as they put it.' When he returned to Carna on 29 March to hand out clothing and tickets to 103 people for the forthcoming voyage, the constabulary had to be called to keep order because of the vast crowds. Georgina Tuke wrote, 'depressed with the sadness and poverty of the place and people'.[50] The Carna area was once again suffering from the failure of the potato leading to the massive demand to leave. Tuke was so moved by the plight of the people that he gave Mr Berry, the relieving officer, £100 to secure meal for the people, and criticized the chief secretary, George Trevelyan, for refusing to allocate relief 'when there is something like starvation in this district'. The demand to be assisted was so great the Tukes had difficulty finishing the interviews.[51] They had to return to conduct further interviews on 2 March and among those who applied were the Foran family, Mathias Geary, Val Kelly and young O'Malley.[52]

The Tuke Committee had initially argued that assistance would initiate chain migration from the region. The basic principle of all assisted emigration schemes in this period was that it helped kick-start the chain migration process from places like Clifden and Oughterard as those sent to North America would send remittances to friends and relations so they could join them.

The Tukes were in Connemara from the 12 February to the 3 March when they left for England, but returned to the task on 16 March. Georgina Tuke's diary and James' correspondence to his daughters, Frances and Meta, from his first marriage, shows they endured a punishing schedule and while long periods were spent examining lists and interviewing applicants, much time was also spent visiting the area. On 28 February, Tuke and Peter King, the relieving officer, came to Creggan, visiting each of the families who had applied, travelling over 50 miles to do so.[53] The administration and bureaucracy involved in the project was immense as the names and other information had to be transcribed onto at least ten official forms. Coordination with the other unions administered by the Tuke Committee was also important so that the transfer to the Allen Line boats could take place. When the *Canadian* left Galway on 21 March for Quebec it had 174 Tuke passengers from Clifden, 54 from Oughterard and 144 from Belmullet, the latter having embarked at Blacksod Bay.[54] However, Tuke was not dejected and observed, 'Poor things it is worth the trouble, and much more to deliver them from our hard woes'.[55] Ten years later, Tuke described the pressures the committee was under: '[We] … recall days of laborious anxiety and "nights devoid of ease" when helping the poor Connemara people to the land of their hearts' desire'.

Besides the challenges of travel, interviews and selection, tight time schedules had to be observed. Between 23 March and 23 June 1883 the committee sent 2,813 emigrants from Galway; 1,589 from Clifden and 1,224 from Oughterard. The first group left on the *Phoenician*. Four days prior to departure the successful emigrants were given the sailing tickets at Letterfrack and the following day 120 were provided with clothing for the journey. Shoes were also given to 160 persons, commissioned from ten shoemakers in Clifden, and they travelled by coach to Galway accompanied by the relieving officers, Peter King and Stephen Joyce. The Clifden and Letterfack groups met at Recess the day before sailing and proceeded to Galway. Among those leaving was Michael Hughes and his family from Letterfrack. In Galway, the emigrants were brought from the docks on the tug, *The City of the Tribes*, and as they boarded the *Phoenician* each person or head of family was given a note for his landing money in Boston which would bring them to their final destination. Prior to sailing they were examined by the shore doctor to ensure they were fit to travel. This was followed on the 31 March by the second group who left on the *Nepigan* and were accompanied by Fr Michael O'Mahony. On 28 April, the committee sent 700 people to North America and 200 came from Clifden and Letterfrack. No sooner had one group left than work was under way with the next. Arrangements had to be made for those leaving from the islands and the remote coastal areas. Those selected from Inishboffin, Roundstone and Carna were brought on the gunboat *Banterer* to sail on the *Manitobian* on the 5 May. It was found that the Carna group was thirty persons short of what had been agreed and it was noted that there were 'evidently some influences at work there'.[56] There were occasions when the Tukes were unable to eat until 10 o'clock at night and then had to deal with money orders, lists, notices to agents in Boston, and other paper work. The pressures can be seen in Tuke's letter to his daughters in May when he said, 'This has been very harrowing work and we are both ragged'.[57] While engaging with the work, Tuke had to contend with food that the Glendalough Hotel in Letterfrack provided and not entirely to his taste. Eggs and bacon were always on the menu and as he did not like the former he had to live on the bacon. Mutton was the other food continuously provided which Tuke found tiresome and on one occasion put it in the fire 'lest Mrs Mullarkey should think I did not rate her cooking'.[58]

Not all of those who applied were selected, for various reasons, in particular the family not having enough members who were breadwinners or did not have a member who was proficient in English. When the interviews took place at Maam on 17 May there were few applicants and nearly all were unsuitable. The application of an ex-policeman, employed on the Mitchell Henry estate as a gardener earning 3s. 6d. a day, was refused. A girl from Carna was turned down because she was in trouble with the law: she had been found in possession of a bottle of poteen and fined 6d. or a term in prison.[59] Applicants were also refused when the constabulary objected: suspects involved in agrarian crime were struck off. When Tuke was carrying out interviews in Letterfrack on 13 March the local police provided a list of those suspected of involvement in recent murders. A boy named Martin Daly was not selected when the crown prosecutor, Mr Henderson, intervened as Daly was wanted as a key witness in the Letterfrack murders that had occurred on 24 April 1881.[60] The refusals did lead to conflict with locals who were providing valuable assistance to Tuke. Revd McAndrew, PP, played a major role in the selections in Letterfrack, but was angry when Widow Joyce and her family were not selected.[61] There were also those who refused to leave even though they were in a destitute state. When Tuke visited The Glen of the Birds near Leenaun on 15 May 1883 no one wanted to go because they had sown their crops and they believed 'they are branded and their children who don't die [are] married to blacks out there'.[62]

The Tuke correspondence relates harrowing accounts of people desperately trying to be included on the lists. He encountered a widow with four children who wanted to be sent to Pittsburgh where she had relatives. She had walked 40 miles to ask for help. She was informed that the last boat which was to leave on 23 June for Boston, the *Waldesian*, was full and the funds were exhausted. Tuke met her again in Oughterard and when she begged him on her knees for help, he was so moved by her story that he decided to pay the fare himself as he had received £12 from a donor in Bristol.[63] The correspondence also highlights unforeseen problems that occurred. When Tuke arrived in Galway on 27 April to send 430 from Connemara on the *Phoenician*, it was discovered that one boy, Connelly, could not travel as he had to be brought to hospital because he had got drunk the previous night and broken his foot.[64]

While the scheme in 1882 had received little public attention, this had changed by 1883. It was inevitable the programme would come into conflict with Irish nationalists. Nugent's scheme to Minnesota in 1880 had been condemned by Charles Stewart Parnell, Michael Davitt and others, which was a major factor in it being discontinued.[65] On his visit to the United States in the spring of 1880, Parnell had refuted the assertion that emigration was the solution to the problems of Irish poverty and congestion. In 1880, Vere Foster wrote to Parnell advocating 'assisted emigration as the most practical and certain mode, not only temporarily but permanently relieving the present poverty and ever recurring distress in the west of Ireland'. He was prepared to subscribe £2 for each man or woman between 18 and 35 years towards an emigration fund.[66] There is no indication that Parnell replied. Both Parnell and Davitt argued that Tuke's scheme was misguided and they were opposed. Their opposition was influenced by the government's involvement, as it was providing the funding.

Nationalists argued for internal migration within Ireland and claimed the government should provide the funding.[67] This was in direct opposition to Tuke who argued that emigration provided the Irish with better opportunities. In this he was proved correct since the Irish Land Purchase and Settlement Company, which was established in 1884 to transfer tenants from congested districts, proved a disaster and while the Bodkin estate at Kilcloony, Co. Galway, was purchased with the purpose of facilitating migration, no land was ever handed over to tenants from outside.[68] While Parnell and Davitt saw Tuke's motives as well intentioned, they felt he was misguided. This was not unexpected and as early as 1881 Tuke realized that the scheme 'would be denounced as a treacherous device for weakening the country'.[69]

By May 1883 there was growing opposition from most nationalist newspapers. Among those was the recently established *United Ireland,* which under the editorship of William O'Brien was outspoken in its language and prepared to attack those who it considered were opposed to the nationalist and Parnellite interests. Within a short while it had the largest newspaper circulation in Ireland and was very influential.[70] As Joseph O'Brien points out there was hypocrisy and inconsistency with *United Ireland*'s criticisms and attacks on Tuke and the government. While O'Brien criticized the government for providing £100,000 at the same time the newspaper carried advertisements for cheap emigration fares to Australia, the United States and Canada.[71] It was also surprising as O'Brien was well aware of the poverty and destitution that prevailed in the west of Ireland having been one of the first to highlight the problem of famine during his tour of Connemara and Mayo in late 1879. Both Tuke and O'Brien had a love of and commitment to the poor of the west and in different ways worked tirelessly to improve their condition. Where they differed was in approach. While O'Brien wanted the people to have ownership of their holdings, Tuke felt their conditions could only be improved through the creation of viable farms by reducing population congestion. In the 1890s, O'Brien was to be a firm supporter of the Congested Districts Board in whose establishment Tuke had played a major role. Tuke described the criticism from the nationalist press as 'very abusive' but it must be noted he was never attacked personally.[72]

Shopkeepers also continued their opposition, worried what would happen the debts they were owed. In March 1883, Tom Sullivan and Stephen Coyne, the latter a publican from Letterfrack, and described by Mrs Tuke as 'a horrid man who never looked you in the face', produced a long list of debtors and what they owed, but none of those selected to emigrate were on it.[73]

When the scheme ended in June 1883 Tuke had assisted 241 families and 300 individuals or parts of families to leave from Clifden union. Of these, 980 went to the United States and settled in twenty states with Minnesota, Pennsylvania and Massachusetts being the main ones. The other 609 went to destinations in Canada. Of those from the Oughterard union, 72 came from the Aran Islands, 322 from Crumpaun, 329 from Lettermore and 224 from Garumna.[74]

In 1883, Tuke published extracts from 53 letters from emigrants who had been assisted in 1882–3 indicating how they were getting on. Twenty of the letters came from Canada, 27 from the United States from those sent in 1883 and six from emigrants assisted in 1882.[75] While the correspondence was published to strengthen the Tuke Committee's case for additional government funding for further emigration projects, the extracts were selective as they mainly highlighted the positive features of their lives in North America. Nevertheless, they indicate the demand for the scheme and the justification for continuing with it. Unfortunately, Tuke only published the initials of the correspondents making it difficult now to identify the individuals involved. At the same time the letters show the spread of destinations where the emigrants settled.

While a fear of the unknown was a deterrent in leaving for Canada in 1882, once letters came back from those who settled there the attitude changed. As Sydney Buxton, who administered the scheme in Belmullet and Newport, said 'the Irish are very much like a flock of sheep, ready blindly to follow if one will lead, but quick to draw back on the slightest alarm'.[76] Those who went to Canada in 1882 were reluctant to settle there because they had no knowledge of the country and few people from Connemara had settled there. They were soon sending glowing reports to friends and relatives of their new lives and this encouraged others from the Clifden union to emigrate to Canada. It was also attractive as in March 1883 the Canadian and Pacific Railway Co. had written to W.H. Smith offering to assist 10,000 Irish families to the country.[77] In 1883, 609 people from Clifden went to Canada and a total of 1,850 were sent by the Tuke Committee from the four unions it administered.[78] Some 650 were sent to Roman Catholic clergymen who promised to look after them, while 1,200 were catered for by agents of the dominion and Ontario governments. All were looked after from the time they disembarked in Quebec to their final destinations, given prepaid rail tickets and helped to find work.[79] Some priests were prepared to accommodate up to six families and provide for them until they settled in. One Connemara family arrived in Peterborough, Ontario, where the local priest agreed to look after them, had a house built for them by the local community, many of them descendants of emigrants assisted from the north Munster region under the Peter Robinson scheme between 1823 and 1825. Other officials rented houses for the emigrants in Hamilton and indicated that work was available for other families if they came.[80] The three families who came to Guelp and the two to Stratford, Ontario, secured employment quickly. About 200 people went to Manitoba, some to Lower Canada and the rest to Ontario. Those who came to Manitoba settled round Winnipeg, were in employment earning between seven and eight shillings a day, while girls were working as domestic servants getting £3 to £4 a month with board.[81] Those who came to the mid-west and Manitoba had higher wages than those who remained in Ontario and along the east coast.

In June 1883, Tuke reflected on the work that had been undertaken over the previous four months and stated, 'the normal misery and discontent springing there from, are ever behind all other things in my mind and form the strongest incentive to continue work in a field which most retire from in disgust or look and pass by on the "other side"'.[82] Even before the large numbers left in 1883 the Tuke Committee felt that more needed to be assisted. Sydney Buxton estimated that along the western seaboard there were between one-quarter and half a million people who were constantly in need of relief and between 25 and 30 per cent should be provided with assistance to North America.[83] On 25 July 1883, the Tuke Committee again petitioned the government and urged the prime minister, William Gladstone, to make further provision for continuing family emigration and it was argued that the demand for emigration would be great.[84] This was supported by others such as the English commentator, George Potter, who said,

> Emigration to be beneficial to the country … must of necessity be aided by the state, for the very classes who the state can best spare are of themselves unable to emigrate from want of the necessary funds.[85]

The Local Government Board's annual report in August 1883 also stated that 'state-aided emigration was exceedingly popular among those it was sought to benefit … Families eagerly availed themselves of the boom offered'.[86] The government was reluctant to break up the machinery that was in place and decided to provide an additional £100,000 for emigration purposes under the Tramways and Public Companies Act. This was subsequently reduced to £50,000 because the Irish Parliamentary Party insisted that an equivalent amount of money be made available for internal migration projects within Ireland. Under the terms of the act, the Tuke Committee extended its operations to include the Swinford poor law union and Arranmore Island off the Donegal coast. The committee now received £8 per emigrant, increased from £5.

It was clear when Tuke commenced the interviews at Letterfrack on 19 February that the demand was not going to be as great as the previous year. As Mrs Tuke observed, 'Nothing like the pressure of last year'. The list for Renvyle contained the names of only nine families and 16 single people, while at Roundstone on 26 February the Tukes interviewed families and a number of single people.[87] Carna and Roundstone were the centres for applications and a large crowd assembled when he arrived in the former, but there were few families and a large number of single people. The demand from single girls was great as there were few employment opportunities in the area and a large number of girls had already been assisted through the Nugent and Vere Foster schemes. These were now sending back positive reports indicating that work was available and wages were good. Bridget Connolly was 18 when she left for Chicago in 1882 and the following year sent money back to her parents as well as the passage fare for her sister who was aged 16. She worked in a restaurant and had secured a position for her sister at £1 a week with food.[88] The evidence from this period indicates that women who emigrated to the United States fared better than men. Employment opportunities were better with most women able to secure positions as domestic servants, or working in mills and the clothing industry. There was always a demand for domestic servants as most American-born women refused to take up these positions because of the long, unsocial hours and poor wages. When the *Phoenician* left Galway on 3 May it included five families from Clonbur, including the widow and five children of Thomas Higgins, who was hanged in 1883 for his part in the Huddy murders.[89]

While Tuke prioritized assisting families, he was not opposed to assisting individuals to leave if they were likely to remit money back to friends and relatives in Connemara. In 1884, while 47 families left from Clifden, another 65 individuals were assisted; 114 families and 73 individuals left from Oughterard.[90] The total assisted from Connemara was 1,116: 347 from Clifden and 769 from Oughterard. They departed on ten ships, the first was the *Grecian*, which left Galway for Boston on 28 March and the last was the *Manitoban*, which sailed from Galway on 13 June with 42 passengers paid for by the Tuke Committee. In 1884, the committee assisted 2,802 people from the five unions under its jurisdiction and they were sent to 148 destinations in the United States and 14 in Canada. Those from Clifden went to 37 locations in the United States, mainly in Minnesota, Wisconsin and the eastern states and to eight destinations in Canada, mainly in Ontario. Those from Oughterard settled in 40 destinations, all in the United States with Pennsylvania the principal state because of the availability of work in the coal mines and iron works, although Minnesota was another major location, in particular St Paul.[91] However, by this stage the days of assisted migration were numbered, but the scheme had achieved its main objective: taking some of the poor and destitute population out of poverty and giving them the opportunity of a better life in North America.

4. Impact of the emigration schemes

By 1884, the Tuke emigration project was coming under pressure from many quarters and finding it increasingly difficult to keep its focus. The hostility was coming from the most powerful sections in Irish society at a national and local level: from the bishops and clergy in the west of Ireland, from Parnell and the Irish Parliamentary Party, and from local merchants and shopkeepers whose political influence at board of guardians level was on the increase. As the whole emigration project was being questioned both inside and outside of parliament, the scheme was under threat. There were questions in parliament as to the state of the emigrants sent from the Belmullet union after a report in a Canadian newspaper that emigrants in Toronto were in a destitute state, and there was criticism from Prof. Thomas Baldwin, who had been assistant commissioner to the Richmond Commission.[1] The greatest threat came from the bishops and sections of the clergy. While the priests in Connemara played an active role in supporting and encouraging emigration in 1882 and 1883, their absence from the interviewing process was noticeable in 1884. In the past the Catholic Church had argued that emigration was a threat to the morals of their people in foreign countries because of the scarcity of priests and churches.[2] This opposition had created major difficulties for schemes such as that of Vere Foster.[3] The death knell for the Tuke scheme was sounded on 5 July 1883 when the bishops passed a resolution against assisted emigration declaring, 'that state-aided emigration as a means of ending this evil (congestion) is unwise and impolitic, and tends only to promote disaffection amongst the Irish at home and abroad'.[4] This was followed in early November 1883 by the clergy of Tuam deanery, comprising 25 clerics and led by Archbishop John McEvilly, stating that emigration should be opposed by every local and constitutional method available. This was after a letter from Archbishop John Lynch of Toronto had been published stating that the assisted emigration schemes be discouraged. It resulted in 97 priests from the archdiocese of Tuam, which encompassed most of Connemara, following this opposition towards assisted emigration.[5]

Tuke found that clerics who had played a major role in previous years were no longer prepared to show their support publicly and those who were opposed in the past were now more vocal in their criticism. While the number of applicants wanting to leave was high, the Tuke Committee found that up to three-quarters of applicants cited various excuses for not going, with opposition from local priests being the main factor.[6] One of the most vocal opponents was Revd Thomas Flannery who in the early stages adopted an ambivalent approach, but by 1884 was hostile. Flannery maintained that as a result of the scheme 250 people from his parish had to enter the workhouse because the young and healthy had gone. When Tuke inquired from John Bourke, the clerk of the Clifden union, he was informed that this was not true.[7] There was also the accusation that the committee was sending out husbands without their wives from Clifden, but it transpired that the wives had already emigrated and the men were only rejoining them.[8] According to Tuke's evidence to the Select Committee on Colonization in 1889, the priests were not opposed to individuals leaving, but did not want the large-scale emigration of families that he was facilitating.[9]

Tuke had started his emigration project in Clifden because of initial support from the local board of guardians, but in time this had turned to hostility. He was able to continue with the scheme because of the help and engagement of the union officials, in particular the relieving officers who played a vital role with the interviews and selection of the suitable candidates. In 1884, the Clifden Board of Guardians passed two resolutions which undermined the viability of the project and indicated the board's position: relieving officers were to discontinue their involvement with the committee's activities and those who failed to do so were to resign their appointments with the board. It meant that people like John Burke, Peter King and Stephen Joyce could no longer provide their services and during the selection of emigrants in 1884, Tuke had to rely on medical officers such as Dr Gorham in Roundstone and Dr Kearney in Carna. Individual guardians acknowledged the benefits of the scheme to the region: one in Clifden, who had opposed the union's decision in 1882 to apply for the loan, wrote to Tuke the following year and stated, 'you have done more to relieve the people of this district than all the relief committees established'.[10] The guardians' hostility towards Tuke was largely influenced by the union's deteriorating financial situation and it argued that by assisting the people to leave it exacerbated its funding problems. Representations were constantly being made to the Local Government Board to provide additional financial assistance and in July 1884 when its debt stood at £2,800 it asked the board to 'press on the government the necessity of coming to our aid with a grant to enable us to tide over the current year'.[11] By this stage the guardians were promoting the construction of a railway line between Galway and Clifden as a solution to the region's problems and an alternative to assisted emigration. J.S. Harvey, who played a major role for the Tuke Committee in Clifden in 1884, was adamant that if the potato failed that year the demand for emigration would be as great as in 1882 and 1883 and 'that no amount of adverse pressure that can be brought to bear will induce the people to remain on holdings which cannot provide them with a bare subsistence'.[12]

However, the harvest of 1883 also influenced the numbers applying to leave. Emigration is influenced by internal and external factors: increasing when economic conditions deteriorate and declining when there is an improvement.

As the potato crop in 1883 was above average throughout Connemara there was not the same pressure on families to leave. Sydney Buxton summed up the situation when he observed that the level of emigration depended on the circumstances of the harvest: if it was bad the numbers looking to leave would be high, but if the crops were good it would lead to fewer seeking assistance to leave.[13]

By the autumn of 1883 there were reports in the Canadian newspapers criticizing the emigrants sent from Ireland. While many of these had been assisted by the poor law unions under the Arrears of Rent Act, no distinction was made between them and those sent by the Tuke Committee.[14] There was a realization from the outset by the Tuke Committee that the schemes administered by the poor law unions did not have the same objectives as vested interests, such as shopkeepers and poor law guardians, who wanted to get rid of long-term problems rather than those best suited for emigration.[15] To ensure that the emigration project was not jeopardized and to counteract the negative publicity, Howard Hodgkins and Major Richard Ruttledge-Fair were sent to Canada and the United States in the autumn of 1883 by the Tuke Committee to investigate the conditions of those aided by the committee. In their report in November 1883, Hodgkins and Ruttledge-Fair stated the position of labourers was far better in Canada than in the eastern or central states of the United States as wages were higher and the cost of living lower. The emigrant who settled in the Boston area was earning 5s. 5d. a day and his board cost 18s. a week, while his counterpart who lived in Peterborough, Ontario, had wages of 5s. 10d. a day and his board cost 12s. a week. They also highlighted that the small towns of Ontario were preferable 'morally and religiously for raw Irish emigrants than the large towns or cities of the eastern or central states of America'. They interviewed one family in St Thomas, Ontario, who were earning $100 a month. Only three of the families assisted by the Tuke Committee were in difficulties. Both representatives were constantly asked by the emigrants to send their friends and families from home. Many of those sent to work with farmers had left, drawn into the small towns and the railway work by the better wages of up to 6s. 3d. a day.[16]

The decision by the Canadian authorities on 31 March 1884 to refuse to accept the emigrants was the main reason why the Tuke Committee discontinued the assisted emigration project the following July. The Canadians were incensed at the way the emigrants sent by the poor law unions were not suitable for settlement: it was felt they were being dumped in North America and would be a burden on the state.[17] While the Canadian memorandum clearly indicated it was the emigrants sent by the unions and not those of the Tuke Committee, it was difficult for Tuke to overturn their decision. The Tuke Committee offered suggestions that would improve the situation such as the inspection of the emigrants before they left Ireland and the appointment of agents to look after the emigrants upon their arrival in Canada, but these were unacceptable to the

authorities. In a letter to Howard Hodgkins, the secretary of the Department of
Immigration, Ontario, David Spence, said

> So far their condition is not encouraging, as many of them are now living
> on charity, and public feeling has been somewhat strongly expressed, in
> the public press and otherwise concerning them. This remark really applies
> to the people sent out by the unions; but they are so closely associated in
> the public mind with some sent out by you, that it will be hard to find
> employment for either class next summer, as the farmers place but little
> value on their labour, and the people of the cities are afraid of laying the
> foundations of pauperism.

The Tuke emigration to Canada scheme suffered because of the perceived
association with the schemes run by the poor law unions. As Lord Brabazon
stated, 'Sending out paupers without proper reference to their character or
physical capabilities, and without finding them employment or providing them
with the means of subsistence on arrival' was a major mistake'.[18] As far as the
general Canadian public was concerned there was no longer any difference
between the carefully planned Tuke scheme and those of the poor law unions
who were using emigration as an opportunity to export a permanent problem.
To Tuke, state-aided emigration could not be successful without the active
participation of colonies like Canada and thus it was decided to discontinue the
scheme. The committee stopped its operations 'while still keeping in existence
the organization of the committee, in view of possible future requirement'.[19]
This indicated that Tuke still believed that emigration from Connemara and
those other unions that the committee was engaged with would be required in
the future. To show how successful the emigration scheme from Connemara
was Tuke published over 200 letters from emigrants, mainly from the Clifden
union, whom the committee had assisted over the previous two years, and stated
that less that 5 per cent of the correspondence was in any way negative. Two
main trends can be observed from these letters: nearly all contained remittances
sent back to family and friends and invariably they urged the recipients to join
them and leave behind the poverty and destitution they were enduring.[20]

The question that has to be asked is, how successful was the Tuke emigration
scheme from Connemara and other parts of the west? The two main objectives of
the project were to assist families to leave so that holdings could be consolidated
and that those who emigrated would remit money back to Connemara to
friends and relatives. According to Tuke in 1889, the first was achieved because
of the 635 holdings that were vacated, 382 were given to adjoining tenants, 161
farms reverted back to the landlords, 36 were taken by new tenants and 56 had
returned to wilderness. All of the land vacated in Clifden had been redistributed
to neighbouring tenants.[21] Despite the large-scale exodus from the Clifden and
Oughterard unions few of the remaining families were in a comfortable position

and it was reported from Oughterard that many were very poor and 'congestion still exists in a serious degree. The people are dependent on the land, and the land as now cultivated, will not support them'.[22] According to John Burke, clerk of the Clifden union, the position of those tenants with small holdings was worse in 1885–6 than it had been in 1879–81.[23] There were some benefits including in Clifden where it led to a rise in wages for agricultural labourers as the supply of labour was reduced. Wages increased from 10*d.* to 1*s.* in 1882 to between 1*s.* 6*d.* to 2*s.* in 1890. By June 1890, Burke indicated that the situation of those who remained in Clifden had improved, while the position of those in North America had greatly improved.[2]

The other objective was that those assisted would send remittances to family and friends which would allow them survive on their small holdings in relative comfort. In 1884, Tuke estimated that those he had sent over the previous two years had remitted between £4,000 and £5,000, with over £2,500 to people in Clifden in sums ranging from £5 to £30, and in one case £40.[25] One of the emigrants who left in rags in 1882 and settled in Pennsylvania sent £20 home over the following two years; while Michael F. who emigrated on the *Canadian* from Galway on 21 May 1883 sent £2 back to his cousin, Tom, in Clifden from Sonk Centre, Manitoba.[26] Another of the Clifden emigrants who was working in a paper mill in Portland, Maine, sent £3 home in July 1883, while remittances between £1 and £4 were sent back from those who settled in Manchester, New Hampshire; Lynn and Boston.[27] One Connemara landowner informed Tuke that all of his tenants had received between £2 and £12 from relatives that had been assisted between 1882 and 1884, and in one case a girl had sent her parents £70.[28] Much of the money sent back came from the large number of single people that had been assisted, in particular from girls. When all of the family left there was not the same pressure to send remittances, but they forwarded money especially during times of crisis as in 1885–6 when the potato once again failed. Tuke also saw that the scheme benefited the local community as the emigrants sent back money to shopkeepers and merchants which paid off old debts.

The money was also used to pay the passage fares of other family members. By 1888, the Tuke emigrants had helped 500 friends and relations to leave from Clifden who otherwise would have been unable to emigrate because of their poverty.[29] One girl who settled in Chicago in November 1883 sent £4 back to her parents and told her sister she would send her the passage fare the following summer so 'father can sit down by the fireside then and let the rough day pass him and us earning lots of money for him in this country where there is plenty of it'. She was earning 16*s.* a week.[30]

The emigrants acted as agents for others to join them through their letters that told of the wages they were earning and how they were progressing. As one of those who settled in Thorn Hill, Ontario, told his friends in Connemara, 'This is a good country. We like it good. Any man can earn money in it. Tell Jim Cauley he can earn lots of money'.[31] P. McC urged his brother and his cousin,

Colman Geary, to come to St Paul 'and not be living in poverty and misery all their life in that country' for 'It is exceedingly bad to have so many stalwart young men and young women waste their lives in Ireland for nothing when in a short time they can accumulate a handsome fortune in America'.[32] Another emigrant based in Wheeling told his friends in Connemara, 'You will be in the midst of luxury and a beautiful continent in the land of freedom … where there is no complaint of miserableness, when every man can run his hand in his pocket and play with those pretty coins called dollars'.[33] One of the emigrants from Oughterard told his sister, 'have courage and don't be a bit afraid coming to this country. Have lots of courage, and come out right off'.[34]

While many correspondents urged their friends and relations to join them so they would have a better life, there were those who were concerned about the conditions their friends and relations endured in Connemara. As one emigrant in St Paul wrote to his friend, 'Take all of your family and don't leave any of them behind you for any money'. The emigrants compared their new circumstances with what they had left and were happy to leave behind the poverty and destitution of Connemara. One of the settlers in Peterborough, Ontario, explained 'Indeed we are glad that we have left that Devil's Den (Ireland) in good time. We are in Heaven now, that is to say, if there is one at all on earth'.[35] Others echoed similar sentiments, like the family from Feenish Island who had settled in Portland, Maine, 'I ain't sorry for leaving Ireland, and if I got Feenish Island free for ever I would not go. There ain't a month but we would have £20 a month'.[36] Revd Michael Mahony who accompanied one of the groups of Tuke emigrants to North America said of those who were in Minnesota, 'If any wish to see old Ireland, it is as American tourists'.[37]

While the early emigrant letters were inevitably positive as they were leaving famine and poverty, their long-term achievements in North America showed the advantages of the emigration scheme from Connemara. A sizeable group of the Tuke emigrants settled in Minnesota as it adhered to the criteria in relation to the mid-west and offered better economic prospects. There was the additional advantage that Bishop John Ireland and the clergy of St Paul were prepared to work with the emigrants, sending them to destinations where there were employment opportunities. Those sent out in 1884 went to 14 destinations in the state including Austin, Minneapolis, Prior Lake and St Paul. The support of the local Catholic clergy can be seen in the intervention of one cleric, Fr F., who gave part of his father's farm to one of the Clifden emigrants.[38] In May 1884, Bishop Ireland told Tuke, 'The emigrants sent out this spring are of a superior class, and must be looked upon as a benefit to the community among which they may cast their lot'.[39]

The emigrants who arrived in St Paul, many from the Carna area, came at a time when there was a major demand for labour as the state was opened by the railway companies. There were employment opportunities as a new rail network was being established and extensive street improvements put in place.

During his visit to the mid-west in the autumn of 1880 Tuke was aware of the problems that the unskilled labourer would encounter – only able to work for seven months of the year because of the severe weather conditions. As a result labourers would have to survive on the wages they earned for those seven months of the year. Despite this handicap, Tuke still felt that life in the mid-west was better for the Connemara emigrant than the poverty and squalor of the industrial cities in the east.[40] The new arrivals in Minnesota from Connemara were helped by former neighbours from home who provided valuable advice, information, guidance and assistance. Revd Michael Mahony stayed in Minnesota and told Tuke in November 1888 that 'I can say that they have been lifted to quite a new life, benefited every way, and are right along doing better and better'.[41] He sent information on fifty of the Tuke emigrants from Connemara who had settled in St Paul, providing details on how the families were doing and the wages they were earning. Nearly all the families had at least one wage earner and in most cases there were several. As a result they had accumulated savings while at the same time were sending money back to relatives in the west of Ireland. One family was earning $116 a month with two of the children working in a shoe factory, while another family had a combined monthly income of $60 a month, part of which came from selling butter and milk from the cows they kept.[42] Three members of another family were working in Ryan's Hotel earning between $12 and $14 a month along with their board. As nearly all of the family was working, the father had purchased a house and a lot for $650, an investment he could never have aspired to had he remained in Connemara.[43] However, for others old habits remained with many of the emigrants in St Paul still renting rather than purchasing their homes, a relic of life back in Connemara when they rented their holdings, and even the houses that they bought were 'often bare, unpartitioned, unplastered, unpapered'. The emigrants were not prepared to spend money extravagantly, but ensured they ate well, probably because of the subsistence experiences they endured in Ireland. They bought the best of food and groceries, in particular meat, suggesting that their improved purchasing power allowed them buy the food of their choice.[44] The sense of community and living close to neighbours from home was important to the emigrants. Many that had been sent to Canada made their way across the border and came to St Paul including one group who had originally settled in Pembroke. They wanted to be close to neighbours from Connemara as it also allowed them to speak the language they were more familiar with, Irish. Others came to Minnesota lured by the better wages.[45]

Not all who left from Connemara left willingly. According to Henry Robinson many of the older people were reluctant emigrants and only left so their sons and daughters could have a better life in North America, but returned to Connemara after their families had settled in the United States.[46] While Sydney Buxton in 1896 acknowledged that a small number did return, but 'the return in nearly every case being due to sickness and when they returned they have come back better off than when they left'.[47]

While the potato harvest was good in 1884, the situation deteriorated greatly the following year and there were fears that Connemara was about to face a famine crisis as the people consumed their seed potatoes. The areas worst affected were Bunowen and Carna, and by May 1886 some 18,000 people in the Clifden union were surviving by working on relief works.[48] In February 1886, Tuke returned to Connemara and was exasperated by the poverty and destitution that he once again witnessed as a result of the failure of the potato. He had been asked by the Gladstone administration to organize a private subscription to purchase seed potatoes for distribution among the small holders of Connemara, Achill and Belmullet. It resulted in £5,200 being collected. Tuke's intervention was significant in averting a crisis with 500 tons of seed potatoes being distributed in Clifden and 20 tons in Carraroe. Many of the witnesses before the Poor Relief Inquiry in 1886 testified that the potatoes provided were instrumental in preventing starvation, while Revd P. Lynskey, PP of Clifden, told Tuke that the people 'frequently come to tell how grateful they have reason to be to you'. Even his old adversary, Revd Thomas Flannery, said, 'I don't know what would become of these people only for you'.[49] Once again Tuke devoted much time and effort to his work telling his daughter, Frances, 'Our work has been terribly hard. Often we are at work until one or two, sometimes as hard as we were with assisted emigration arrangements', and on another occasion commented, 'The work grows more onerous ... The poverty is unspeakable – and what misery and suffering are borne which are never revealed until some stranger comes poking into these out of the way corners'.[50] In 1886, Tuke made his views known in a letter, that everybody was aware of the problems and difficulties of the small holders in the region, but nobody was prepared to provide any long-term intervention, 'the necessity for action is acknowledged, and the question is what shall that action be?'[51] Once again he argued that emigration was the preferable option for the people of Connemara and £500,000 would allow 50,000 people 'be placed in a position to earn large wages in the Greater Britain of our colonies or in the United States'. He was opposed to the internal migration of tenants with small holdings to other parts of Ireland for even if a person was transferred to twenty acres of ordinary land he would barely raise himself above the position of a well-paid labourer.[52] Even though £15,000 remained unused for emigration from the 1883 Public Companies and Tramways Act, Tuke made a number of applications after 1884 to have the money released, but this was refused by the government. In 1885 and 1886, Tuke received applications from a large number of people for assistance to emigrate and he privately provided the funds for more than one hundred people to leave for North America. Again in 1890 when there was another crisis with the potato, he contributed towards another 80 people to migrate from Clifden.[53]

As late as 1890 Tuke was still advocating assisted emigration as a remedy for the poverty of Connemara and suggesting that it should be available to those who wanted to leave. He argued, 'the proportion leaving the congested districts is owing to the poverty of the people'. He estimated that 100,000 families still lived in extreme poverty and that at least one-fifth needed to be helped to emigrate so that the remaining families could live in relative comfort. Again he referred to Connemara because the resources of the region could not sustain the existing population for 'so long as thousands of the people are attempting to live on an acre and a-half to two acres of bog land, it is evident that if the crops fail, they must again be thrown into distress'.[54] Tuke even questioned the propriety of the Ashbourne Land Purchase Act, which provided government loans so farmers could purchase their farms, maintaining it would do little for places like Connemara, 'should we not merely be face to face with 300,000 impoverished owners instead of 300,000 impoverished tenants'.[55]

Tuke was aware that emigration alone was not the solution to the poverty, destitution and repeated famines associated with Connemara and the other congested districts, but the development of its economic resources also needed to take place. In 1881 and again in 1886 after he visited Connemara and Mayo when recommending relief, he also stated that fishing be encouraged as well as the provision of a light railway between Galway and Clifden.[56] Within a year of Tuke's visit to Connemara to distribute the seed potatoes the new Conservative administration under its new Irish chief secretary, Arthur Balfour, was acknowledging that the congested districts were an issue that had to be dealt with.[57] This resulted in a consultation with Tuke as to how this could be achieved and ultimately led to the establishment of the Congested Districts Board in 1891. Tuke was nominated as a member of the committee and over the next five years he devoted his time and energy to implementing and advancing its policies. While one of its objectives included the provision of an assisted emigration scheme, at Tuke's insistence, it was never activated because of the opposition of Irish nationalists.

Conclusion

The 1880s and 1890s were a period of challenges and change for an Ireland dominated by political, agrarian and economic issues. The subsistence crises that occurred in Connemara and elsewhere during these decades were largely overshadowed in the newspapers by national events such as the Land League agitation, the rise of Parnell, the 1886 Home Rule bill, and the split in the Irish Parliamentary Party as a result of the Parnell divorce case. As a result, the periodic failures of the potato crop and near starvation position of communities along the west coast did not receive the attention that they deserved and it was left to an English philanthropist to champion their plight and make radical proposals as to a solution.

Between 1882 and 1884 the Tuke Committee helped 4,946 people to emigrate from Connemara, representing 12 per cent of the local population. Not since the Great Famine had there been such a major exodus from a region over such a short period. 3,230 people emigrated from the Clifden union, accounting for about 500 families and some single people, while 1,716 people came from Oughterard. The total cost of the project in the five unions administered by the Tuke Committee was nearly £70,000. While the government provided £44,500, the Tuke Committee contributed £20,000; the rest coming mainly from the Duchess of Marlborough Relief Fund (£3,600), with the emigrants and their friends coming up with £1,400. The average cost per person of sending out an emigrant was £7 6s.[1] In most cases the emigrants contributed nothing.

James Hack Tuke must be seen as a man ahead of his time for as early as the 1840s when he first visited Ireland he realized that major changes needed to be implemented in order for the people of Connemara and other parts of the west of Ireland to live in relative comfort. While assisting the poor to emigrate had been attempted during the Great Famine, Tuke's approach was more radical in that it was targeted at the most destitute and congested parts of the country. He argued government intervention was required to create this change and when this was not forthcoming he initiated the private emigration scheme. Tuke's suggestions as to government intervention in economic matters were novel. Those who advocated such approaches in the past had neither the persistence nor influence to create this transformation. One of Tuke's contemporaries said of him that he took pains to acquire the practical knowledge of the questions that he desired to deal with and had the gift of being forcible and lucid in expressing his views. As a result 'he was able largely to influence and to shape the social policy of successive governments in dealing with the poor parts of

Ireland'.[2] In September 1886, the duke of Bedford, who had always supported Tuke's endeavours, told him that emigration was the saviour of Ireland and 'it succeeds when undertaken by a man of power like yourself, animated by a sense of duty'.[3] His political contacts were important in pursuing his objectives for the poor of the west of Ireland as seen in 1883 when he persuaded the government to provide the financial assistance required for emigration. He had close connections with the political establishment in both the Liberal and Conservative parties, in particular with successive Irish chief secretaries such as W.E. Forster, George Trevelyan, John Morley and Arthur Balfour. Consequently, he was able to achieve his goals such as the assisted emigration scheme and the establishment of the Congested Districts Board. The political establishment in Britain was prepared to engage with him and seek his advice because he was impartial and had no political agenda. His dedication and focus helped him to improve the social and economic position of the people of Connemara and other poor parts of the west. Through his unbiased approach he was able to gain the confidence of the people of Connemara and their leaders who came to realize that he was an outsider who could be trusted and who had a deep sympathy with them. This work was also acknowledged by the establishment in Britain, but Tuke did not seek rewards or accolades for his work for the poor of Ireland and Sir William Gregory described him as 'Ireland's greatest benefactor'. He refused the offer of a knighthood from Earl Spencer in recognition of his work for the poor in Ireland.[4]

Throughout his dealings with the poor, Tuke showed great organizational skills, determination and strong convictions in relation to what he was doing. To send over 9,500 people to varied destinations in North America was a major achievement and in particular when he faced such powerful opposition within Ireland. The assisted emigration scheme's success could only be achieved with the assistance of friends and associates who came to help him in Connemara and elsewhere. These included Major Ruttledge-Fair, Howard Hodgkins and Major W. Gaskell. From the time the scheme was started in 1882, to the distribution of seed potatoes during the distress of 1885–6 and engagement with the Congested Districts Board after 1891, these friends worked closely with Tuke in his endeavours to improve the position of the people in the west of Ireland.

The Tuke emigration scheme from Connemara was successful because it was carefully planned and implemented: only one or two families from each electoral division was sent on each shipment to avoid local opposition while only a small number of families was sent to each destination in North America so that they would secure employment and avoid criticism from the local population. The schemes ensured that families were not broken up and in some cases helped unite them: many girls had left Connemara under the Vere Foster scheme and the Tuke project allowed the rest of the family to join them.

The emigrants who left between 1882 and 1884 were not a homogenous group and like all who leave, had different reasons for emigrating and each had their own story to tell. Mrs Conroy had returned from the United States after nine months so that she could bring out her five children and in May 1884 applied to the committee to be assisted. Mrs Nee wanted to join her husband in south Boston along with her six children. He had sent £15 towards the passage costs of the family, but she had to apply to the committee for the entire family to leave and they sailed on the *Phoenician* on 23 March 1883. Others applied who had returned from the States and now wanted to be sent back as with Thomas Earles from Carna.[5] Long after the scheme ended Tuke found that the people of Connemara appreciated what he had done. In 1893, Tuke came across a man named Folan and when he heard that the committee had helped his relation, John Folan, to leave for America, he took off his hat and said, 'Then it is you we ought to be cheering'.[6]

     While the emigration project was not the total solution to the problems of Connemara, it was an important component in the long-term strategy to alleviate the issues of poverty, destitution and population congestion. The transfer of the distressed and poor population was a short-term solution and Tuke acknowledged that other remedial measures needed to be put in place for the remaining population. As Connemara continued to suffer from crop failures throughout the 1880s and 1890s, the fact that nearly 5,000 of its inhabitants had emigrated under the Tuke scheme meant the number suffering from distress was lower than it would otherwise have been. Those who were assisted now came to the aid of those who remained in Connemara through remittances that helped purchase food and also through the provision of pre-paid passage fares to North America. The exertions of the Tuke Committee led to chain migration from the region to the United States and Canada, which previously had not been in place because of the poverty of the people and their inability to fund their emigration. Tuke's scheme helped to kick-start emigration which led to others being given the opportunity to leave. Even when they settled abroad the sense of community and loyalty remained strong leading to the establishment of Connemara communities in the United States and Canada: from Carna to St Paul, from Cois Fharraige to Portland, Maine, from Clifden to Pittsburgh. Though many were happy to leave behind poverty and the perennial threat of famine, their sense of place remained strong. It was Tuke's foresight and determination between 1882 and 1884 that offered the poor of Connemara an opportunity of a better life in North America.

Notes

ABBREVIATIONS

DCA Dublin City Archives
DDA Dublin Diocesan Archives
NLI National Library of Ireland
UL University of Limerick

INTRODUCTION

1 William Makepeace Thackeray, *The Irish sketchbook, 1842* (1843, repr. Belfast, 1985), pp 205–29; *Hall's Ireland: Mr and Mrs Hall's tour of Ireland* (1841, repr. London, 1984), pp 411–19; Glenn Hooper (ed.), *Harriet Martineau: letters from Ireland* (Dublin, 2001), pp 80–4.

2 David Fitzpatrick, *Oceans of consolation: personal accounts of Irish migration to Australia* (Ithaca, NY, 1994), pp 3–36.

3 Quoted in Gerard Moran, 'Farewell to Kilkelly, Ireland: emigration from post-famine Mayo' in Gerard Moran & Nollaig Ó Muraile (eds), *Mayo: history and society* (Dublin, 2014), p. 395.

4 David Fitzpatrick, 'Irish emigration in the later nineteenth century', *Irish Historical Studies*, 22:86 (Sept. 1880), 126.

5 Maureen Murphy (ed.), *Your fondest Annie: letters from Annie O'Donnell to James P. Phelan, 1901–4* (Dublin, 2005), pp 2–3; see also pp 36–7.

6 See Gerard Moran, ' "Shovelling out the poor": the Irish poor law and assisted emigration during the Great Famine' in Ciarán Reilly (ed.), *The famine Irish: emigration and the Great Hunger* (Dublin, 2016), pp 22–40.

7 Gerard Moran, *Sending out Ireland's poor: assisted emigration from Ireland in the nineteenth century* (Dublin, 2004), pp 28–34.

8 Wendy Cameron, 'Peter Robinson's settlers in Peterborough' in Robert O'Driscoll and Lorna Reynold (eds), *The untold story: the Irish in Canada* (Toronto, 1988), pp 343–54.

9 Moran, *Sending out Ireland's poor*, p. 80.

10 Oliver MacDonagh, 'Irish emigration to the United States of America and the British colonies during the great famine' in R. Dudley Edwards & T. Desmond Williams (eds), *The Great Famine: studies in Irish history, 1848–52* (1956, rep. Dublin, 1994), pp 332–9.

11 Ciara Breathnach, *The Congested Districts Board of Ireland, 1891–1922: poverty and development in the west of Ireland* (Dublin, 2005), pp 21–2.

1. CONNEMARA AND THE 'FORGOTTEN FAMINE', 1879–81

1 *The agricultural statistics of Ireland for the year 1881*, HC 1881, lxxiv (c 3332), pp 19–20.

2 *Emigration from Ireland; being the second report of 'Mr Tuke's Fund'* (London, 1883), p. 11.

3 J.H. Tuke, 'Ought emigration from Ireland to be assisted', *Contemporary Review* (April 1882), 700.

4 *Emigration from Ireland; being the second report of 'Mr Tuke's Fund'* (London, 1884), p. 29.

5 *Report of the select committee on colonization, together with the proceedings of the committee, minutes of evidence and appendix*, HC 1890, xii (345), p. 205, q. 3427.

6 *Third report of 'Mr Tuke's Fund'*, p. 30.

7 Kathleen Villiers-Tuthill, *Beyond the Twelve Bens: a history of Clifden and district, 1860–1923* (Clifden, 1986), p. 37.

8 Tuke, 'Ought emigration be assisted', p. 698.

9   Villiers-Tuthill, *Beyond the Twelve Bens*, p. 37. In 1867, the amount advanced by the agents towards the kelp was £3,000.

10 J.H. Tuke, *Irish distress and its remedies, the land question: a visit to Donegal and Connaught in the spring of 1880* (London, 1880), pp 76–7.

11 T.P. O'Neill, 'Minor famines and relief in Galway, 1815–1925' in Gerard Moran (ed.), *Galway: history and society* (Dublin, 1996), p. 463.

12 Ibid.

13 *Report of the Mansion House Relief Committee for the relief of distress in Ireland* (Dublin, 1862).

14 Villiers-Tuthill, *Beyond the Twelve Bens*, pp 35–7; Clifden Poor Law Union minute book, dated June 1867 (Galway County Library, Clifden Poor Law Union minute books).

15 Henry Robinson, *Memories; wise and otherwise* (Dublin, 1924), p. 13.

16 J.W. Allies to Edward McCabe, dated 2 Jan. 1880 (DDA, McCabe papers, laity 1880).

17 *The Irish crisis of 1879–80: proceedings of the Mansion House Relief Committee* (Dublin, 1881), p. 2.

18 *Relief of distress on the west coast of Ireland*, HC 1880, lxii (c 2671), p. 2.

19 Catherine Jennings, 'Tuke: the Quaker philanthropist and the free emigration scheme in Connemara, 1882' in Gearóid Ó Tuathaigh et al., *Mr Tuke's Fund: Connemara emigration in the 1880s* (Clifden, 2014); Tuke, *Irish distress and its remedies*, p. 25.

20 *Irish crisis of 1879–80*, p. 8.

21 For the role of the clergy in the crisis of 1879–81 see Gerard Moran, 'Near famine: the Roman Catholic Church and the subsistence crisis of 1879–82', *Studia Hibernica*, 32 (2002–3), 155–78.

22 *Galway Vindicator*, 8 Feb. 1879.

23 Gerard Moran, 'From Great famine to forgotten famine: the crisis of 1879–81' in Patrick Fitzgerald, Christine Kinealy & Gerard Moran (eds), *Irish hunger and migration: myth, memory and memorialization* (Quinnipiac, 2015), pp 122–3.

24 *Galway Vindicator*, 18 June 1879.

25 Ibid., 8 Nov. 1879.

26 *Connaught Telegraph*, 5 July 1879.

27 Mitchell Henry, 'The distress in Ireland', *Dublin Review* (Apr. 1880), p. 467.

28 *Galway Vindicator*, 13 Sept. 1879; *Nation*, 20 Sept. 1879.

29 Villiers-Tuthill, *Beyond the Twelve Bens*, p. 50.

30 *Galway Vindicator*, 31 Dec. 1879.

31 Reprinted in *Boston Pilot*, 8 May 1880.

32 Quoted in *Connaught Telegraph*, 18 Oct. 1879.

33 See Brendan O'Donoghue, *Activities wise and otherwise: the career of Sir Henry Augustus Robinson* (Dublin, 2015), pp 17–18.

34 Jennings, 'Tuke … the Quaker philanthropist', p. 35; O'Neill, op. cit., p. 466; *Connaught Telegraph*, 27 Nov. 1879.

35 *Galway Vindicator*, 12 Nov. 1879; *Connaught Telegraph*, 15 Nov. 1879; N.D. Palmer, *The Irish Land League crisis* (repr. New York, 1978), p. 78.

36 *Irish crisis of 1879–80*, p. 10.

37 Ibid., pp 9–10.

38 Many Irish newspapers, such as the *Nation*, opposed the giving out of relief stating what Ireland needed was not charity, but public works, see *The Nation*, 27 Dec. 1879.

39 See duchess of Marlborough letter to the *Times*, reprinted in *Galway Vindicator*, 20 Dec. 1879; Tuke, *Irish distress and its remedies*, p. 64.

40 *Irish crisis, 1879–80*, p. 15. Among those involved in collecting donations in Australia was Charles Gavan Duffy.

41 Minutes of meeting, dated 3 Jan. 1880 (DCA, Mansion House Relief Committee Papers, ch1/4).

42 *Galway Vindicator*, 6 Dec. 1879.

43 *Connaught Telegraph*, 3 Jan. 1880; *Nation*, 10 Jan. 1880; *Irish World*, 31 Jan. 1880.

44 Minutes of meeting dated 13 Jan. 1880 (DCA, Mansion House Relief Committee papers, 1880, ch1/4).

45 Dublin Mansion House Relief Committee for the relief of distress in Ireland, dated 2 Jan. 1880 (DDA, McCabe papers, secular priests, 1880).

46 J.A. Fox, *Reports on the condition of the peasantry of the county of Mayo, during the famine crisis of 1880* (Dublin, 1880), p. 9.

47 See Gerard Moran, 'From Galway to North America: state-aided emigration

from County Galway in the 1880s' in Moran (ed.), *Galway: history and society*, p. 488.

48 Tuke, *Irish distress and its remedies*, p. 74; for an account of the religious tensions in Connemara between the Irish Church Mission Society and the Catholic Church see Villiers-Tuthill, *Beyond the Twelve Bens*, pp 48–55; Miriam Moffitt, *Soupers and jumpers: the Protestant missions in Connemara, 1848–1937* (Dublin, 2008), pp 135–51,

49 *The Nation*, 10 Jan. 1880.

50 Minutes of meeting of 9 Mar. 1880 (DCA, Mansion House Relief Committee papers, 1880, ch1/4).

51 Tuke, *Irish distress and its remedies*, p. 79.

52 Palmer, *Land League crisis*, pp 89, 101.

53 Robinson, *Memories: wise and otherwise*, p. 10; O'Donoghue, *Activities wise and otherwise*, p. 18.

54 Tuke, *Irish distress and its remedies*, pp 74, 76–7.

55 Ibid., pp 117–18.

56 See Mansion House Relief Committee papers (DCA, Mansion House Relief Committee papers, ch/1/3). The committee held its last meeting on 9 Sept. 1880.

57 Fr P. Mannion to the Mansion House Relief Committee, dated 30 May 1880 (DCA, Mansion House Relief Committee papers, ch1/260/280).

58 Tuke, *Irish distress and its remedies*, pp 75–6.

59 *Freeman's Journal*, 4 Feb. 1880.

60 E.H. Allies to McCabe, dated 21 Apr. 1880 (DDA, McCabe papers, laity, 1880); MacHale to McCabe, dated 21 Apr. 1880 (ibid., relief of distress papers, 1880).

61 *Relief of distress on the west coast of Ireland*, pp 1–5.

62 Clifden Poor Law Union Archive, 1849–1921 (Galway, 2012), pp xi–xii.

63 *Annual report of the Local Government Board for Ireland, being the ninth report under the Local Government Board (Ireland) Act*, HC 1881, xviii (c 2926), p.80.

64 *Connaught Telegraph*, 19 June 1880.

65 *Irish crisis of 1879–80*, p. 1.

2. JAMES HACK TUKE'S TOUR OF THE WEST OF IRELAND

1 Robinson, *Memories: wise and otherwise*, p. 34; *Select committee on colonization*, p. 200, q. 3404.

2 Helen Hatton, *The largest amount of good: Quaker relief in Ireland, 1654–1921* (Montreal, 1993), p. 180.

3 Quoted in Christine Kinealy, *This great calamity: the Irish Famine, 1845–52* (Dublin, 1994), p. 126.

4 Sir Edward Fry, *James Hack Tuke: a memoir* (London, 1899), pp 77–8.

5 Ibid., pp 82–3.

6 Tuke, *Irish distress and its remedies*, p. vi.

7 Ibid., pp 119–21.

8 Ibid., p, 13

9 Ibid., p. 34.

10 Ibid., pp 84–99.

11 Tuke to Frances and Meta Tuke, dated 22 July 1882 (UL, Tuke papers).

12 O'Donoghue, *Activities wise and otherwise*, pp 20–1; *Connaught Telegraph*, 3 Jan. 1880.

13 *Report into the commission of inquiry into the workings of the landlord and tenant (Ireland) act, 1879 and the amending acts, with evidence, appendices and index* (Bessborough commission), HC 1881 (2779), xviii, p. 652.

14 J.H. Tuke, 'Peasant proprietorship at home', *Nineteenth Century*, 8 (Aug. 1880), 187.

15 Ibid., p. 108.

16 Sydney Buxton, 'Mr Tuke and his work', *Contemporary Review*, 69 (June 1896), 863.

17 Tuke, *Irish distress and its remedies*, p. 34; J.H. Tuke, 'With the emigrants', *Nineteenth Century*, 12 (July 1882), 134.

18 Tuke, *Irish distress and its remedies*, pp 92–3, 42–3.

19 For the Nugent emigration scheme to Minnesota see Gerard Moran, '"In search of the promised land": the Connemara colonization scheme to Minnesota, 1880', *Eire/Ireland*, 31:3–4 (1996), 117–29.

20 Tuke, *Irish distress and its remedies*, p. 109.

21 Ibid., p. 114.

22 *Bessborough commission*, ii, HC 1881 (2779-i), xviii, p. 543, q. 17,710.

23 Fry, *Tuke: a memoir*, pp 134–5.

24 See Gerard Moran, *Sending out Ireland's poor*, pp 170–1; J.H. Tuke, 'Ought

emigration from Ireland to be assisted',
Contemporary Review (Apr. 1882), 702.

25 Lord Brabazon, 'State-directed
emigration: its necessity', *Nineteenth
Century*, 79 (July 1884), 772.

26 Tuke, 'Ought emigration be assisted', 707.

27 Ibid., 702–3.

28 Moran, 'The Connemara colonization
scheme to Minnesota'.

29 For the Sweetman scheme, see Malcolm
Campbell, 'Immigrants on the land: Irish
rural settlement in Minnesota and New
South Wales, 1830–1890', *New Hibernia
Review* (Spring, 1998), 43–61.

30 Ruth-Ann M. Harris, 'Where the poor
man is not crushed down to exalt the
aristocrat: Vere Foster's programme of
assisted emigration in the aftermath of
the Irish Famine' in Patrick O'Sullivan
(ed.), *The Irish world wide: history, heritage,
identity, vi: the meaning of the Famine*
(London and Washington, 1997), pp
172–94.

31 Tuke, 'Ought emigration to be assisted',
701–2; Buxton, 'Tuke and his work',
pp 864–5.

32 Buxton, 'Tuke and his work', p. 865.

33 *Select committee on colonization*, p. 202,
q. 3417.

34 *Reports and papers relating to 'Mr Tuke's
Fund'*, p. 25.

35 Ibid., p. 53.

36 Buxton, 'Tuke and his work', p. 866.

3. TUKE AND THE EMIGRATION SCHEMES
FROM CONNEMARA

1 Tuke to Frances and Meta Tuke, dated 5
Apr. 1882 (UL, Tuke Papers).

2 Tuke, 'Ought emigration to be assisted',
p. 703.

3 *Poor Law (Ireland) inquiry commission,
report and evidence with appendices*, HC
1887, xxxviii (c 5043), p. 147, q. 7082.

4 Tuke to Frances Tuke, dated 16 Apr.
1882 (UL, Tuke papers)

5 Fry, *Tuke: a memoir*, pp 138–9.

6 *Reports and papers relating to 'Mr Tuke's
Fund'*, pp 41–2.

7 Tuke to Frances Tuke, undated (UL,
Tuke papers).

8 Tuke to Meta Tuke, 12 Apr. 1882 (UL,
Tuke papers).

9 *Reports and papers relating to 'Mr Tuke's
Fund'*, p. 43.

10 *Select committee on colonization*, p. 202,
qs 3419–20.

11 Mr Vere Foster's second emigration
female fund, 1880–3 (NLI, MS 13,552,
William O'Brien papers).

12 Tuke, 'Ought emigration be assisted', p.
703; Tuke to Meta Tuke, dated 18 Apr.
1882 (UL, Tuke papers).

13 Tuke to his daughters, dated 27 Feb. 1882
(UL, Tuke papers).

14 Fry: *Tuke: a memoir*, pp 147–8.

15 For an account of the evictions see
Villiers-Tuthill, *Beyond the Twelve Bens*,
pp 57–60.

16 *The Nation*, 10 June 1882.

17 Tuke to Frances Tuke, undated (UL,
Tuke papers).

18 Tuke to Meta Tuke, dated 12 Apr. 1882
UL, Tuke papers.

19 *Reports and papers relating to 'Mr Tuke's
Fund'*, pp 31–2.

20 Clifden Poor Law Union archives,
1849–1921 (Galway, 2010).

21 Tuke to Meta Tuke, dated 18 Apr. 1882
(UL, Tuke papers).

22 See Moran, *Sending out Ireland's poor*,
pp 35–69.

23 Tuke to Meta Tuke, dated 12 Apr. 1882
(UL, Tuke papers).

24 *Poor relief (Ireland) inquiry commission*,
p. 126, qs 6068–70.

25 Tuke to Frances and Meta Tuke, dated 5
Apr. 1882 (UL, Tuke papers).

26 Tuke to his children, dated April 1882,
(UL, Tuke papers).

27 Letter of W.P. Gaskell, dated 12 June
1882 in *Reports and papers relating to 'Mr
Tuke's Fund'*, p. 50.

28 Ibid., p. 42.

29 Tuke to Frances Tuke, undated 1882
(UL, Tuke papers).

30 Tuke to Frances and Meta Tuke, undated
1882 (UL, Tuke papers).

31 *Reports and papers relating to 'Mr Tuke's
Fund'*, p. 20.

32 Ibid., p. 50.

33 Ibid., p. 46.

34 Ibid., p. 32.

35 Ibid., p. 46.

36 Georgina Kennedy Tuke diary, entry
dated 21 Feb. 1883 (NLI, MS49,529/90,
John Pitt Kennedy papers).

37 Buxton, 'Tuke and his work', pp 866–7.
38 *Reports and papers relating to 'Mr Tuke's Fund'*, pp 56–7.
39 Tuke to Frances Tuke, undated 1882 (UL, Tuke paperes).
40 Tuke to Meta Tuke, dated 28 July 1882 (UL, Tuke papers).
41 Tuke to Frances and Meta Tuke, undated 1882 (UL, Tuke papers).
42 Robinson, *Memories: wise and otherwise*, p. 29.
43 Buxton, 'Tuke and his work', p. 867.
44 *Emigration from Ireland; being the second report of the committee of 'Mr Tuke's Fund'* (London, 1883), p.6.
45 Tuke to Meta Tuke, dated 26 July 1882 (UL, Tuke papers).
46 *Annual report of the Local Government Board for Ireland, being the thirteenth report under the Local Government Board (Ireland) Act*, HC 1884–5, xxxiv (c 4400), p. 85; *Reports and papers relating to 'Mr Tuke's Fund'*, p. 61.
47 Georgina Tuke diary, dated 12 Feb. 1883 (NLI, MS 49.529/90, John Pitt Kennedy papers).
48 Georgina Tuke diary, entry dated 22 Feb. 1883 (NLI, MS 49,529/90, John Pitt Kennedy papers); Fry, *Tuke: A memoir*, pp 170–1. The boat that left on 23 March was the *Phoenician*.
49 Tuke diary, entry dated 19 Feb. 1883.
50 Ibid., entry dated 23 Mar. 1883.
51 Ibid., entries dated 27 Feb. & 3 Apr. 1883.
52 Ibid., entry dated 2 Mar. 1883.
53 Ibid., entry dated 28 Feb. 1883.
54 *Emigration from Ireland; being the second report of 'Mr Tuke's Fund'*, p. 4.
55 Tuke to Frances Tuke, undated, Sunday 1883 (UL, Tuke papers).
56 Georgina Tuke diary, entry dated 4 May 1883.
57 Tuke to Frances and Meta Tuke, dated 9 May 1883 (UL, Tuke papers).
58 Tuke to Frances, undated (UL, Tuke papers).
59 Georgina Tuke diary, entries dated 17 May, 18 Feb. 1883 (NLI, MS 49,529/90, John Pitt Kennedy papers).
60 Fry, *Tuke: a memoir*, pp 171–3; Georgina Tuke diary, dated 27 Apr. 1883 (NLI, MS 49,529/90, John Pitt Kennedy papers). For an account of the Letterfrack murders see Villiers-Tuthill, *Beyond the Twelve Bens*, pp 66–79.
61 Tuke diary, entry dated 19 Feb. 1882 (NLI, MS 49,529/90, John Pitt Kennedy papers).
62 Ibid., entry dated 15 May 1883.
63 Tuke to Meta Tuke, dated July 1883 (UL, Tuke papers).
64 Georgina Tuke diary, entry dated 27 Apr. 1882 (NLI, MS 49,529/90, John Pitt Kennedy papers).
65 Moran, 'Connemara colonization scheme to Minnesota, 1880', pp 139–41.
66 Mary McNeill, *Vere Foster, 1819–1900: an Irish benefactor* (Belfast, 1971), pp 190–1.
67 Lawrence Marley, *Michael Davitt: freelance radical and frondeur* (Dublin, 2007), pp 141–2.
68 See Gerard Moran, 'The Irish Land Purchase and Settlement Company and the attempted migration scheme to Kilcloony in the 1880s', *Irish Economic and Social History*, 32 (2005), 47–62.
69 Tuke, 'Irish emigration', pp 370–1.
70 See Sally Warwick-Haller, *William O'Brien and the Irish land war* (Dublin, 1990), pp 43–54; Myles Dungan, *Mr Parnell's rottweiler: censorship and the United Ireland newspaper, 1881–1891* (Dublin, 2014).
71 Joseph V. O'Brien, *William O'Brien and the course of Irish politics, 1881–1918* (Berkeley, 1976), p. 17.
72 Tuke to Frances Tuke, undated 1883 (UL, Tuke papers).
73 Tuke diary, entry dated 19 Mar. 1883 (UL Tuke papers).
74 *Second report of 'Mr Tuke's Fund'*, p. 44.
75 *Reports and papers relating to 'Mr Tuke's Fund'*, pp 107–18.
76 Buxton, 'A new exodus', p. 885.
77 Georgina Tuke diary, entry dated 3 Mar. 1883 (UL Tuke papers).
78 *Second report of the committee of 'Mr Tuke's Fund'*, pp 11–12.
79 Lord Brabazon, 'State-directed emigration: its necessity', *Nineteenth Century*, 86 (July 1884), 781.
80 For the Peter Robinson scheme to Peterborough, Ontario see Moran, *Sending out Ireland's poor*, pp 21–8; , *Reports and papers relating to 'Mr Tuke's Fund'*, pp 112–13.
81 *Reports and papers relating to 'Mr Tuke's Fund'*, p. 128.

82 Tuke to unknown, dated 10 June 1883
(UL, Tuke papers).

83 Buxton, 'A new exodus', pp 885–6.

84 *Reports and papers relating to 'Mr Tuke's
Fund'*, p. 104.

85 Brabazon, 'State-directed emigration',
p. 781.

86 *Annual report of the Local Government Board
for Ireland, being the twelfth report under the
Local Government Board (Ireland) Act*, HC
1884, xxxviii (c 4051), p. 50.

87 Georgina Tuke diary, entries dated 20
and 28 Feb. 1884 (NLI, MS 49,529/90,
John Pitt Kennedy papers). For
the role of Thomas Higgins in the
Huddy murders see, Jarlath Waldron,
Maamtrasna: the murders and the mystery,
(Dublin, 1992), pp 220–2.

88 Ibid., entry dated 6 May 1884.

89 Ibid, entries dated 4 & 9 May 1884.

90 *Emigration from Ireland; being the third
report of the committee of 'Mr Tuke's Fund'*
(London, 1884), p. 29, 36.

91 Ibid., pp 8–9, 29, 36.

4. IMPACT OF THE EMIGRATION
SCHEMES

1 Georgina Tuke diary, entry dated 22
Feb. 1884 (NLI, MS 49,529/90, John Pitt
Kennedy papers); *Nation*, 1 Dec. 1883.

2 See Patrick O'Farrell, 'Emigrant
attitudes and behaviour as a source for
Irish history', in G.A. Hayes McCoy
(ed.), *Historical Studies*, x (Galway, 1976),
pp 123–4; see also *Tuam News*, 5 Oct.
1883.

3 McNeill, *Vere Foster*, pp 197–8.

4 Fry, *Tuke: a memoir*, p. 197.

5 *Connaught Telegraph*, 10 Nov. 1883;
Galway Vindicator, 10 Nov. 1883.

6 *Select committee on colonization*, p. 213, q.
3574.

7 Fry, *Tuke: a memoir*, pp 179–80; Tuke
diary, entry dated 28 Feb. 1884.

8 Tuke diary, entry dated 1 Mar. 1883.

9 *Select committee on colonization*, p. 210,
q. 3504–5.

10 *Reports and proceedings of 'Mr Tuke's Fund'*,
p.15

11 Clifden Poor Law Union Archive
Collection, 1849–1921, pp xii–xiii.

12 *Third report of the committee of 'Mr Tuke's
Fund'*, p. 37.

13 Buxton, 'A new exodus', p. 885.

14 See Gerard Moran, 'State-aided
emigration from Ireland to Canada in the
1880s', *Canadian Journal of Irish Studies*,
20:2 (Dec. 1994), 1–19.

15 Buxton, 'A new exodus', p. 886.

16 *Reports and proceedings of 'Mr Tuke's Fund'*,
pp 128–32.

17 Brabazon, 'State-directed emigration',
p. 775.

18 Ibid., pp 774–6.

19 *Third report of the committee of 'Mr Tuke's
Fund'*, pp 3–4.

20 Ibid., p. 12.

21 *Select committee on colonization*, pp 203–4,
q. 3428.

22 *Third report of the committee of 'Mr Tuke's
Fund'*, p. 31.

23 *Poor relief (Ireland) inquiry; reports and
evidence with appendices*, HC 1887, xxxviii
(c-5043), p. 156, qs 7484–5.

24 *Select committee on colonization*, p. 207, qs.
3460–1; p. 203, q. 3416.

25 Ibid., p. 203, q. 3427.

26 *Third report of the committee of 'Mr Tuke's
Fund'*, p. 23, 28.

27 *Reports and proceedings of 'Mr Tuke's Fund'*,
p. 115.

28 Ibid., p. 271.

29 *Select committee on colonization*, p. 203, qs.
3427.

30 *Third report of the committee of 'Mr Tuke's
Fund'*, pp 25–6.

31 *Reports and proceedings of the 'Mr Tuke's
Fund'*, p. 108.

32 *Third report of the committee of 'Mr Tuke's
Fund'*, p. 23.

33 Buxton, 'Mr Tuke and his work', pp
873–4.

34 *Third report of the committee of 'Mr Tuke's
Fund'*, p. 32.

35 Ibid., pp 24, 26.

36 *Reports and proceedings of the 'Mr Tuke's
Fund'*, p. 113.

37 Ibid., p. 177.

38 Ibid., p. 270.

39 *Third report of the committee of 'Mr Tuke's
Fund'*, p. 15.

40 Tuke, 'Irish emigration', pp 361–2.

41 *Select committee on colonization*, p. 203, qs.
3415.

42 *Reports and proceedings of 'Mr Tuke's Fund'*,
p. 265.

43 Ibid., p. 269.

44 *Reports and proceedings of 'Mr Tuke's Fund'*, p. 267.
45 Michael Mahony, 'With the Connemara emigrants in St Paul, Minnesota' in *Reports and proceedings of the 'Mr Tuke's Fund'*, p. 5.
46 Robinson, *Memories: wise and otherwise*, pp 52–3.
47 Buxton, 'Mr Tuke and his work', p. 876.
48 *Poor relief (Ireland) inquiry*, p. 151, q. 7275.
49 *Reports and proceedings of the 'Mr Tuke's Fund'*, p. 12.
50 Tuke to Frances Tuke, dated 25 Apr. 1886; to Meta Tuke, dated 17 Apr. 1886 (UL, Tuke papers).
51 J.H. Tuke, 'Suggestions for the improvement of the congested districts of Ireland, written in 1886' in *Reports and proceedings of 'Mr Tuke's Fund'*, p. 257.
52 *Reports and proceedings of 'Mr Tuke's Fund'*, p. 190; *Select committee on colonization*, p. 204, qs. 3429.
53 Tuke, 'Suggestions for the improvement of the congested districts', p. 261.
54 J.H. Tuke, 'The condition of Donegal' in *Reports and proceedings of 'Mr Tuke's Fund'*, p. 255; *Select committee on colonization*, p. 205, q. 3441.
55 Quoted in Carla King, 'Our destitute countrymen on the western coast: relief and development strategies in the congested districts in the 1880s and 1890s' in Carla King and Conor McNamara (eds), *The west of Ireland: new perspectives on the nineteenth century* (Dublin, 2011), p. 170.
56 Fry, *Tuke: a memoir*, p. 248.
57 Blanche Dugdale, *Arthur James Balfour*, i (London, 1936), p. 128.

CONCLUSION

1 *Reports and papers relating to the proceedings of 'Mr Tuke's Fund'*, p. 88.
2 Buxton, 'Tuke and his work', p. 860.
3 Fry, *Tuke: a memoir*, pp 220–1.
4 Ibid., p. 221.
5 Tuke diary, entries dated 9 Mar. 1884 & 28 Feb. 1883 NLI, MS 49,529/90, John Pitt Kennedy papers).
6 Tuke to Meta Tuke, dated 13 Aug. 1893 (UL, Tuke papers).